Introduction
to Traffic Engineering
交通工程专业导论

徐锦强　黄海南　编著

中国建筑工业出版社

图书在版编目（CIP）数据

交通工程专业导论 = Introduction to Traffic
Engineering：英文 / 徐锦强，黄海南编著. — 北京：
中国建筑工业出版社，2023.12（2025.8重印）
ISBN 978-7-112-29550-0

Ⅰ.①交… Ⅱ.①徐…②黄… Ⅲ.①交通工程—英
文 Ⅳ.①U491

中国国家版本馆CIP数据核字（2023）第253766号

责任编辑：孙书妍　李玲洁
责任校对：王　烨

Introduction to Traffic Engineering
交通工程专业导论
徐锦强　黄海南　编著
*
中国建筑工业出版社出版、发行（北京海淀三里河路9号）
各地新华书店、建筑书店经销
北京锋尚制版有限公司制版
建工社（河北）印刷有限公司印刷
*
开本：787 毫米×1092 毫米　1/16　印张：7　字数：170 千字
2023 年 12 月第一版　　2025 年 8 月第二次印刷
定价：**38.00** 元
ISBN 978-7-112-29550-0
（42041）

Preface

The transportation system is often referred to as the nation's "lifeblood circulation system". Without the ability to travel and to transport goods, society must be structured around small self-sufficient communities, each of which produces food and material for all of its needs locally and disposes of its wastes in a similar manner. The benefits of economic specialization and mass production are possible only where transportation exists to move needed materials for production to centralized locations, and finished products to widely dispersed consumers.

Referring to domestic and foreign traffic engineering textbooks, traffic engineering standards and norms, this book systematically and briefly introduces the basic concepts, theories and methods of traffic systems, which covers the key research content and research methods of traffic engineering and other essential introductory knowledge. This book is mainly written in English, suitable for domestic undergraduate students majoring in traffic engineering, and also suitable for foreign readers to understand the characteristics of the traffic system in China. The book is organized into seven major functional parts:

- Chapter 1—Introduction to Traffic Engineering
- Chapter 2—Road User and Vehicle Characteristics
- Chapter 3—Traffic Stream Characteristics
- Chapter 4—Traffic Control Devices
- Chapter 5—Traffic Management
- Chapter 6—Transportation Planning
- Chapter 7—Intelligent Transportation System

Each chapter consists of four parts: text, exercises, glossary and the key points. In the text, the traffic engineering professional words are highlighted in italic and bold form, which are explained in Chinese at the glossary part at the end of each chapter. Furthermore, some unusual words (underlined in the text) are also given Chinese definitions to make them easier for readers to understand.

This book is mainly written by Associate Professor Jinqiang Xu and Lecturer Hainan Huang of Fujian Agriculture and Forestry University. Associate Prof. Xu wrote the first and seventh chapters, and Lecturer Huang wrote the second to sixth chapters. In addition, master students such as Jieling Huang, Zhenghang Shen, Yangfeng Gong, Xiuwei Lin, Siqi Wu, Cheng Xu, Zeyu Wu and Jiaxin Wen in the research group participated in part of the writing work.

The text is funded by the construction fund of Fujian Province's First-class Undergraduate Major (Traffic Engineering).

In the process of writing this book, a large number of domestic and foreign books and documents have been referred to, and we would like to express our high respect and heartfelt thanks to the authors. Due to our limited knowledge, it is inevitable that there will be mistakes and omissions in the text. Please do not hesitate to contact us with your advices.

Jinqiang Xu, Hainan Huang
August 5th, 2023

前言

    交通运输系统时常被誉为一个国家运行的"血液循环系统"。如果失去人员出行和运送货物的能力，社会将被局限于一个自给自足的小社区，所有需要的食物、材料及其废弃物都将限于当地小社区。只有当交通系统能够运输需要的生产材料到集中加工的区域，并将产品转运给消费者，社会经济专业化和大规模的生产活动才有可能开展。

    本书参考国内外交通工程学教材、交通工程标准和规范，系统且简要地介绍了交通运输系统的基本概念、理论及方法，涵盖了交通工程专业的重点研究内容、研究方法等导论必备知识。本书主要采用英文编写，适用于国内交通工程专业本科学生入门学习和使用，也适用于国外读者了解中国交通系统的特点。全书主要由7个章节组成：

- 第1章 交通工程简介；
- 第2章 道路用户和车辆特性；
- 第3章 交通流特性；
- 第4章 交通控制设施；
- 第5章 交通管理；
- 第6章 交通规划；
- 第7章 智能交通系统。

    每个章节由正文、练习、专业词汇和本章要点4个部分组成。正文中，交通工程专业词汇采用了斜体、加粗的形式进行强调，且在每章后面的"专业词汇"中给出中文释义。同时为便于读者阅读，正文中出现的较生僻词汇（下划线标示）也会给出中文释义。

    本书由福建农林大学徐锦强副教授和黄海南讲师主笔，徐锦强副教授编写了第1章和第7章，黄海南讲师编写了第2章至第6章的内容。此外，课题组黄洁玲、沈正航、龚扬峰、林休玮、吴思琦、徐成、吴泽宇和温家欣等硕士研究生共同参与了部分编写工作。

本书由福建省一流本科专业（交通工程）建设经费资助出版。

本书在研究与编写过程中参考了国内外大量书籍、文献，在此谨向文献作者表示崇高的敬意与衷心的感谢！由于编者水平有限，书中难免有错漏之处，恳请读者批评指正，特此致谢！

徐锦强　黄海南

2023年8月5日

Contents

Chapter 3

Traffic Stream Characteristics   37

Chapter 1 Introduction to Traffic Engineering

1.1   Traffic Engineering as a Profession

The Institute of Transportation Engineers defines traffic engineering as a subset of transportation engineering as follows.

Transportation engineering (交通运输工程) is the application of technology and scientific principles to the planning, functional design, operation, and management of facilities for any mode of transportation in order to provide for the safe, rapid, comfortable, convenient, economical, and environmentally compatible movement of people and goods.

Traffic engineering (交通工程) is that phase of transportation engineering which deals with the planning, geometric design and traffic operations of roads, streets, and highways, their networks, terminals, abutting lands, and relationships with other modes of transportation.

These definitions represent a broadening of the profession to include multimodal transportation systems and options, and to include a variety of objectives in addition to the traditional goals of safety and efficiency.

The key objectives of the definitions of traffic engineering include safety, speed, comfort, convenience, economy, and environmental compatibility.

1.1.1   Safety: The Primary Objective

The principal goal of the traffic engineering remains the provision of a safe system for highway traffic. This is no small concern. In recent years, fatalities on US highways have ranged between 40,000 and 43,000 per year. More Americans have been killed on US highways than in all of the wars in which the nation has participated, including the Civil War. In China, highway fatalities reached over 60,000 per year in the past decade.

While total highway fatalities per year have remained relatively constant over the past two decades, accident rates based on vehicle-miles traveled have consistently declined. Improvements in fatality rates reflect a number of trends, many of which traffic engineers have been instrumental (有帮助的) in implementing.

Stronger efforts to remove dangerous drivers from the road have yielded significant dividends in safety. Driving under the influence (*DUI*,饮酒驾驶) and driving while intoxicated (*DWI*,醉酒驾驶) offenses are more strictly enforced, and licenses are suspended or revoked more easily as a result of DUI/DWI convictions, poor accident record, and/or poor violations record.

Vehicle design has greatly improved. Today's vehicles feature padded dashboards, collapsible steering columns, seat belts with shoulder harnesses, air bags (some vehicles now have as many as eight), and antilock braking systems.

Highway design has been improved through the development and use of advanced barrier systems for medians and roadside areas.

Traffic control systems communicate better and faster, and surveillance systems can alert authorities to accidents and breakdowns in the system.

1.1.2   Other Objectives

The definitions of transportation and traffic engineering highlight additional objectives: speed, comfort, convenience, economy and environmental compatibility, most of which are self-evident desires of the traveler. All of these objectives are also relative and must be balanced against each other and against the primary objective of safety.

While the speed of travel is much to be desired, it is limited by transportation technology, human characteristics, and the need to provide safety. Comfort and convenience are generic terms and mean different things to different people. Comfort involves the physical characteristics of vehicles and roadways, and is influenced by our perception of safety. Convenience relates more to the ease with which trips are made and the ability of transport systems to accommodate all of our travel needs at appropriate times. Economy is also relative. There is little in modern transportation systems that can be termed "cheap". Highway and other transportation systems involve massive construction, maintenance and operating expenditures, most of which are provided through general and user taxes and fees. Nevertheless, every engineer, regardless of discipline, is called on to provide the best possible systems for the money.

Harmony with the environment is a complex issue that has become more important over time. All transportation systems have some negative impacts on the environment. All produce air and noise pollution in some forms, and all utilize valuable land resources. In many modern cities, transportation systems utilize as much as 25% of the total land area. "Harmony" is achieved when transportation systems are designed to minimize negative environmental impacts, and where system architecture provides for <u>aesthetically</u> (审美地) pleasing facilities that "fit in" with their surroundings.

The traffic engineer is tasked with all of these goals and objectives and with making the appropriate tradeoffs to optimize both the transportation system and the use of public funds to build, maintain, and operate them.

1.2   Transportation Systems and their Functions

Transportation systems are a major component of the economy and have an enormous impact on the shape of the society and the efficiency of the economy in general.

Table 1.1   Development of Transportation Infrastructure in China

Year	2012*	2019	2022	Unit
Highspeed Railway Mileage	1.0	3.5	4.2	10^4km
Expressway Mileage	9.6	15.0	17.73	
Inland Waterway Mileage	12.5	12.7	12.8	
Postal & Express Network Mileage	1092.0	4085.9	6012.9	
Number of Civil Airports	183	238	254	—
Number of Port Berths ($\geqslant$ 10,000 t)	1886	2520	2751	—

* Data of items in 2012 and 2019 from Reference [18].

According to the "White Paper on Sustainable Transport Development in China", mileages of highspeed railway, expressway, inland waterway, and postal and express network have been steadily developed, indicated in Table 1.1. The number of civil airports and port berths ($\geqslant$10,000 t) increased by 38.8% and 45.8%, respectively, from 2012 to 2022.

1.2.1   The Nature of Transportation Demand

Transportation demand is directly related to land-use patterns and to available transportation systems and facilities. Figure 1.1 illustrates the fundamental relationship which is circular and ongoing. Transportation demand is generated by the types, amounts, and intensity of land use, as well as its location. The daily journey to work, for example, is dictated by the locations of the worker's residence and employer and the times that the worker is on duty.

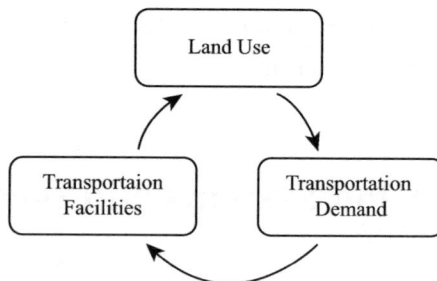

Figure 1.1   The Nature of Transportation Demand

Transportation planners and traffic engineers attempt to provide capacity for observed or predicted travel demand by building transportation systems. The improvement of transportation systems, however, makes the adjacent and nearby lands more accessible and, therefore, more attractive for development. Thus, building new transportation facilities leads to further increases in land-use development, which (in turn) results in even higher transportation demands. This circular, self-reinforcing characteristic of traffic demand creates a central dilemma: building additional transportation capacity invariably leads to incrementally increased travel demands.

In many major cities, this has led to the search for more efficient transportation systems, such as public transit and car-pooling programs. In some of the largest cities, providing additional system capacity on highways is no longer an objective, because such systems are already substantially choking in congestion. In these places, the emphasis shifts to improvements within existing highway rights-of-way and to the elimination of bottleneck locations (without adding to overall capacity). Other approaches include staggered work hours and workdays to reduce peak hour demands, and even more radical approaches involve development of satellite centers outside of the central business district (CBD) to spatially disperse (疏散) highly directional demands into and out of city centers.

Demand, however, is not constrained by capacity in all cities, and the normal process of attempting to accommodate demand as it increases is feasible in these areas. At the same time, the circular nature of the travel/demand relationship will lead to congestion if care is not taken to manage both capacity and demand to keep them within tolerable limits.

It is important that the traffic engineer understands this process. It is complex and cannot be stopped at any moment in time. Demand-prediction techniques (not covered in this text) must start and stop at arbitrary points in time. The real process is ongoing, and as new or improved facilities are provided, travel demand is constantly changing. Plans and proposals must recognize both this reality and the professional's inability to precisely predict its impacts. A 10-year traffic demand forecast that comes within approximately ±20% of the actual value is considered a significant success. The essential truth, however, is that traffic engineers cannot simply build their way out of congestion.

1.2.2 Concepts of Mobility and Accessibility

Transportation systems provide the nation's population with both mobility and accessibility. The two concepts are strongly interrelated but have distinctly different elements. *Mobility* refers to the ability to travel to many different destinations, while *accessibility* refers to the ability to gain entry to a particular site or area.

Mobility emphasizes the through movement of people, goods, and vehicles from point A to point B in the system and gives travelers a wide range of choices as to where to go to satisfy particular needs. Mobility allows shoppers to choose from among many competing shopping centers and stores. Similarly, mobility provides the traveler with many choices for all kinds of trip purposes, including recreational trips, medical trips, educational trips, and even the commute to work. The range of available choices is enabled by having an effective transportation network that connects to many alternative trip destinations within a reasonable time, with relative ease, and at reasonable cost.

Accessibility denotes the direct connection to abutting lands or development such as home, stores, schools, office buildings etc., and is a major factor in the value of land. When land can be accessed by many travelers from many potential origins, it is more desirable for development and, therefore, more valuable. Thus, proximity (靠近) of land to major highways and public transportation facilities is a major factor determining its value.

Mobility and accessibility may also refer to different portions of a typical trip. Mobility focuses on the through portion of trips and is most affected by the effectiveness of through facilities that take a traveler from one general area to another. Accessibility requires the ability to make a transfer from the transportation system to the particular land parcel on which the desired activity is taking place. Accessibility, therefore, relies heavily on transfer facilities, which include parking for vehicles, public transit stops, and loading zones.

A good transportation system must provide for both mobility and accessibility and should be designed to separate the functions to the extent possible to ensure both safety and efficiency. Relationship between mobility and accessibility is shown in Figure 1.2, from which we can see that with an increase of mobility, the ability to access any development decreases, and vise versa.

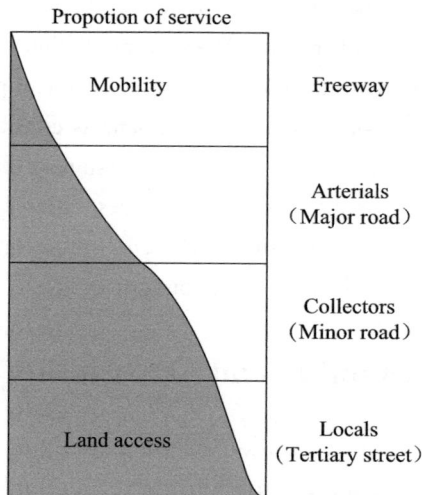

Figure 1.2   Relationship of Mobility versus Accessibility

1.2.3   Components of Traffic Systems

To begin to understand the functional and operational aspects of traffic on streets and highways, it is important to understand how the various elements of a traffic system interact. Further, the characteristics of traffic streams are heavily influenced by the characteristics and limitations of each of these elements. There are four critical components that interact in a traffic system:

- road users—drivers, pedestrians, bicyclists, and passengers;
- vehicles—private and commercial;
- streets and highways;
- the general environment.

The success of traffic engineering depends upon the coordination among the four primary components above. Their characteristics are major factors which affect the design of traffic engineering and the performance of the traffic system. To provide an efficient and safe traffic system, knowledge of the characteristics of these components is essential, like driver characteristics, passenger characteristics, pedestrian characteristics, vehicle characteristics, and roadway characteristics. It is also important to analyze the interrelationships among these components in order to determine the effects.

The most common unit used by the traffic engineer is "vehicles". Highway systems are planned, designed, and operated to move vehicles safely and efficiently from place to place. Yet the movement of vehicles is not the objective; the goal is the movement of the people and goods that occupy vehicles.

Modern traffic engineering now focuses more on people and goods. Although lanes must be added to a freeway to increase its capacity to carry vehicles, its person-capacity can be increased by increasing the average vehicle occupancy. Consider a freeway lane with a capacity of 2,000 vehicles per hour (vehs/h). If each vehicle carries one person, the lane has a capacity of 2,000 persons/h as well. If the average car occupancy is increased to 2.0 persons/veh, the capacity in terms of people is doubled to 4,000 persons/h. If the lane were established as an exclusive bus lane, the vehicle-capacity might be reduced to 1,000 vehs/h due to the larger size and poorer operating characteristics of buses as compared with automobiles. However, if each bus carries 50 passengers, the people-capacity of the lane is increased to 50,000 persons/h.

The efficient movement of goods is also vital to the general economy of the nation. The benefits of centralized and specialized production of various products are possible only if raw materials can be efficiently shipped to manufacturing sites and finished products can be efficiently distributed throughout the nation and the world for consumption. Although long-distance shipment of goods and raw materials is often accomplished by water, rail, or air transportation, the final leg of the trip to deliver a good to the local store or the home of an individual consumer generally takes place on a truck using the highway system. Part of the accessibility function is the provision of facilities that allow trucks to be loaded and unloaded with minimal disruption to through traffic and the accessibility of people to a given site.

The general environment also has an impact on traffic operations, but this is difficult to assess in any given situation. Such factors as weather, lighting, density of development, and local enforcement policies all play a role in affecting traffic operations. These factors are most often considered qualitatively, with occasional supplemental quantitative information available to assist in making judgments.

1.2.4 Classification of Highways

In order to have highways provide different services in terms of mobility and accessibility, it is necessary to stratify (层次化) the roadway system. In general hierarchy of highway classification is made based on traffic mobility and land access level. High-class highways have a high-level of mobility whereas low-class highways have a high-level of accessibility. Freeways provide a high-level of mobility whereas local streets provide the best access to land development.

Different countries have their own roadway classification based on their situations. All highway systems involve a hierarchal classification by the mix of mobility and accessibility functions provided. In the USA, they divide the highway system into four major classes: freeways, arterials, collectors, and local streets. For different locations, the classification can be different. In China, there are five classes for rural highways. They are freeways, first-class highways, second-class highways, third-class highways and fourth-class highways. For urban roadway, there are also five categories. They are freeways, expressways, major streets, minor streets, and tertiary (or local) streets (Table 1.2).

Table 1.2 Classifications of Highways in China and the United States

China		United States	
Urban	**Rural**	**Urban**	**Rural**
Freeway	Freeway	Freeway	Interstate
Expressway	1st Class Highway	—	—
Arterial	2nd Class Highway	Arterial	Primary
Collector	3rd Class Highway	Collector	Secondary
Local Street	4th Class Highway	Local	Tertiary

1.2.5 *Transportation Modes*

Although the traffic engineer deals primarily with highways and highway vehicles, there are other important transportation systems that must be integrated into a cohesive (团结的) national, regional, and local transportation network. Table 1.3 provides a comprehensive listing of various transportation modes and their principal uses.

The traffic engineer deals with all of these modes in a number of ways. All over-the-road modes—automobile, bus transit, trucking—are principal users of highway systems. Highway access to rail and air terminals is critical to their effectiveness, as is the design of specific transfer facilities for both people and freight. General access, internal circulation, parking, pedestrian areas, and terminals for both people and freight are all projects requiring the expertise of the traffic engineer.

Moreover, the effective integration of multimodal transportation systems is a major goal in maximizing efficiency and minimizing costs associated with all forms of travel.

Table 1.3   Transportation Modes

Type	Mode	
Urban People-transportation Systems	Automobile Taxi/For-hire Vehicles Bus Transit Light Rail Heavy Rail	Non-motor vehicles (Bicycles and Electric Bicycles) Para-transit (Ferry, Cableway, Pedicab, etc.)
Intercity People-transportation Systems	Automobile Intercity Bus Railroad	Air Water
Urban and Intercity Freight Transportation	Long-haul Trucks Local Trucks Railroad	Water Air Freight Pipelines

1.3   Elements of Traffic Engineering

There are a number of key elements of traffic engineering:

(1) traffic studies and characteristics;

(2) performance evaluation;

(3) facility design;

(4) traffic control;

(5) traffic operations;

(6) transportation systems management;

(7) integration of intelligent transportation system technologies.

Traffic studies and characteristics involve measuring and quantifying various aspects of highway traffic. Studies focus on data collection and analysis that is used to characterize traffic, including (but not limited to) traffic volumes and demands, speed and travel time, delay, accidents, origins and destinations, modal use, and other variables.

Performance evaluation is a means by which traffic engineers can rate the operating characteristics of individual sections of facilities and facilities as a whole in relative terms. Such evaluation relies on measures of performance quality and is often stated in terms of "levels of service". Levels of service are letter grades, from A to D, describing how well a facility is operating using specified performance criteria. Like grades in a course, A is very good, while D connotes failure (on some level). As part of performance evaluation, the capacity of highway facilities must be determined.

Facility design involves traffic engineers in the functional and geometric design of highways and other traffic facilities. Traffic engineers are not involved in the structural design of highway facilities but should have some appreciation for structural characteristics of their facilities.

Traffic control is a central function of traffic engineers and involves the establishment of traffic regulations and their communication with the driver through the use of driver control devices, such as signs, markings, and signals.

Traffic operations involve measures that influence overall operation of traffic facilities, such as one-way street systems, transit operations, curb (控制) management, and surveillance (监测) and network control systems.

Transportation systems management (*TSM*) involves virtually all aspects of traffic engineering with a focus on optimizing system capacity and operations. Specific aspects of TSM include high-occupancy vehicle priority systems, car-pooling programs, pricing strategies to manage demand, and similar functions.

Intelligent transportation systems (*ITS*) refers to the application of modern telecommunications technology to the operation and control of transportation systems. Such systems include automated highways, automated toll-collection systems, vehicle-tracking systems, in-vehicle GPS and mapping systems, automated enforcement of traffic lights and speed laws, smart control devices, and others. This is a rapidly emerging family of technologies with the potential to radically alter the way we travel as well as the way in which transportation professionals gather information and control facilities. While the technology continues to expand, society will grapple with the substantial (大量的) "big brother" issues that such systems invariably create.

1.4 Modern Problems for Traffic Engineers

We live in a complex and rapidly developing world. Consequently, the problems that traffic engineers are involved in evolve rapidly.

While safety is an important consideration in many human activities, it has a particularly prominent role in transportation. Every type of transportation system involves some risk of harm, as has been the case since antiquity (古代), and seems likely to remain the case in the future. More than a million people are killed on the world's roads each year. Statistics, reported by Forbes News, showed that an estimated 38,680 people were killed in traffic accidents in the United State in 2020, up 7.2 percent from 36,096 in 2019 and the highest number in 13 years. The US National Highway Traffic Safety Administration (NHTSA, 美国国家公路交通安全管理局) cited dangerous driving, speeding and failure to wear seat belts as major factors in the increase. The injuries and death numbers caused by traffic accidents remind us of the traffic safety problem has become one of the primary aspects of our social health problems.

Urban congestion has been a major issue for many years. Given the transportation demand cycle, it is not always possible to solve congestion problems through expansion of capacity. Traffic engineers therefore are involved in the development of programs and strategies to manage demand in both time and space and to discourage growth where necessary. A real question is not "how much capacity is needed to handle demand?" but rather, "how many vehicles and/or people can be allowed to enter congested areas within designated time periods?"

Environmental impacts have become one of the most important challenges to the traffic system. Based on environmental impact scoping, the large-scale impacts due to the system as a whole include air quality, energy consumption, and land use. The small-scale impacts due to specific transportation facilities and activities include those related to the displacement of residents and businesses due to construction of transportation facilities, noises, impacts on wildlife, impacts on water quality, visual impacts, temporary impacts during construction, and impacts resulting from construction of transportation facilities in environmentally sensitive areas.

The list goes on and on. The point is that traffic engineers cannot expect to practice their profession only in traditional ways on traditional projects. Like any professional, the traffic engineer must be ready to face current problems and to play an important role in any situation that involves transportation and/or traffic systems.

Exercises

1. Define traffic engineering and transportation engineering. What are the basic differences between transportation engineering and traffic engineering?
2. Define mobility and accessibility, and describe the relationship between mobility and accessibility.
3. What are the parts of the transportation system?
4. What are the modes of transportation?
5. What are the classifications of roadways in China?
6. What are the basic contents of traffic engineering study?
7. Describe modern problems for traffic engineers.

Glossary

1. *Transportation engineering*: 交通运输工程，将技术和科学原理应用于交通运输方式及设施的规划、功能设计、运行和管理，以提供人员和货物的安全、快速、舒适、方便、经济和环保的运输。

2. *Traffic engineering*: 交通工程学，是交通运输工程的分支，研究道路规划、几何设计、交通管理和道路网、起终点站、毗邻用地与各种交通方式的关系。

3. *DUI*: *driving under the influence,* 饮酒驾驶，车辆驾驶人员血液中的酒精含量大于或者等于20 mg/100 mL，小于80 mg/100 mL的驾驶行为。

4. *DWI*: *driving while intoxicated,* 醉酒驾驶，车辆驾驶人员血液中的酒精含量大于或者等于80 mg/100 mL的驾驶行为。

5. *Transportation systems*: 交通系统，由人、车、路、设施、管理、环境等许多子系统组成的综合性整体；其各子系统从属于这个整体，而整个交通系统又是更庞大的城市系统的子系统。

6. *Transportation demand*: 交通需求，指交通系统用户的出行意愿。

7. *Mobility*: 机动性，指到达不同目的地的能力；机动性是对出行方式的时间便捷性的度量。

8. *Accessibility*: 可达性，指进入特定区域或场所的能力；可达性是对出行场所的空间便捷性的度量。

9. *Transportation modes*: 交通方式，即出行方式，涵盖步行、非机动车、公共交通、轨道交通、小汽车、大客车、航空、水运等不同方式。

10. *Traffic characteristics*: 交通特性，即道路交通系统各基本要素（人、车、路）的自身特性以及各要素之间的相关特性。

11. *Performance evaluation*: 性能评估，在现有或规划的交通需求下，通过通行能力与服务水平分析，可以发现交通设施存在的问题，并寻找解决问题的方法，正确评价道路运行状况，为制定正确的交通管理措施提供依据。

12. *Facility design*: 交通设施设计，指对交通安全设施、交通管理设施、道路通信系统、收费系统、监控系统、静态交通设施、交通服务设施、道路照明设施、交通环保设施等进行设计。

13. *Traffic control*: 交通控制，运用各种控制软硬件设备，如人工、交通信号、电子计算机、可变标志等手段来合理地指挥和控制交通。

14. *Traffic operations*: 交通运营，指交通系统的运行和经营，通过交通法规、行政管理、工程技术管理、交通信号控制技术等方面的综合技术应用，实现交通系统的安全、有序、通畅和可持续发展等运行目标。

15. *Transportation system management (TSM)*: 交通系统管理，指通过改善车辆和道路的管理、运营来实现更有效地利用现有的交通设施。

16. *Intelligent transportation system (ITS)*: 智能交通系统，指以全方位提升交通运输效率与安全性、促进交通运输可持续发展为主要目的，综合运用先进的传感技术、计算机技术、电子控制技术及信息与通信技术等现代高科技，整合多模式交通管理策略，建立起来的一种以智能化为主要特征，实时、准确、高效的交通运输管理系统。

Key Points

1. Briefly describe the definition of traffic engineering and the relations between traffic engineering and transportation engineering.
   简述交通工程学定义及其与交通运输工程的关系。
2. Briefly describe the purposes of traffic engineering.
   简述交通工程学的目的。
3. Briefly describe the basic composition and basic concepts of the transportation system.
   简述交通系统基本组成和基本概念。
4. Briefly describe the main research objects of traffic engineering.
   简述交通工程学主要研究对象。
5. Briefly describe the problems of modern transportation system.
   简述现代交通系统的问题。

Chapter 2 Road User and Vehicle Characteristics

Although traffic engineers have little control over driver and vehicle characteristics, design of roadway systems and traffic controls is in the core of their professional practice. In both cases, a strong degree of uniformity of approach is desirable. Roadways of a similar type and function should have a familiar "look" to drivers; traffic control devices should be as uniform as possible. Traffic engineers strive to provide information to drivers in uniform ways. Although this does not assure uniform reactions from drivers, it at least narrows the range of behavior as drivers become accustomed to and familiar with the cues traffic engineers design into the system.

2.1   Road User Characteristics

Human beings are complex and have a wide range of characteristics that can and do influence the driving task. In a system where the driver is in complete control of vehicle operations, good traffic engineering requires a keen understanding of driver characteristics. Much of the task of traffic engineers is to find ways to provide drivers with information in a clear, effective manner that induces safe and proper responses.

The two driver characteristics of utmost importance are visual acuity factors and the reaction process. The two overlap in that reaction requires the use of vision for most driving cues. Understanding how information is received and processed is a key element in the design of roadways and controls.

There are other important characteristics as well. Hearing is an important element in the driving task (i.e., horns, emergency vehicle sirens, brakes squealing, etc.). Although noting this is important, no traffic element can be designed around audio cues because hearing-impaired and even deaf drivers are licensed. Physical strength may have been important in the past, but the evolution of power-steering and power-braking systems has eliminated this as a major issue, with the possible exception of professional drivers of trucks, buses, and other heavy vehicles.

Of course, one of the most important human factors that influences driving is the personality and psychology of the driver. This, however, is not easily quantified and is difficult to consider in design. It is dealt with primarily through enforcement and licensing procedures that attempt to remove or restrict drivers who periodically display inappropriate tendencies, as indicated by accident and violation experience.

2.1.1   Visual Characteristics of Drivers

When drivers initially apply for, or renew, their licenses, they are asked to take an eye test, administered either by the state motor vehicle agency or by an optometrist or ophthalmologist who fills out an appropriate form for the motor vehicle agency. The test administered is a standard chart-reading exercise that measures ***static visual acuity***, that is, the ability to see small stationary details clearly.

(1) Visual Factors in Driving

Although static visual acuity is certainly an important characteristic, it is hardly the only visual factor involved in the driving task. The Traffic Engineering Handbook provides an excellent summary of visual factors involved in driving, as shown in Table 2.1.

Many of the other factors listed in Table 2.1 reflect the dynamic nature of the driving task and the fact that most objects to be viewed by drivers are in relative motion with respect to the driver's eyes.

Because static visual acuity is the only one of these many visual factors examined as a prerequisite to issuing a driver's license, traffic engineers must expect and deal with significant variation in many of the other visual characteristics of drivers.

Table 2.1　Visual Factors in the Driving Task

Visual Factor	Definition	Sample Related Driving Task (s)
Accommodation	Change in the shape of the lens to bring images into focus	Changing focus from dashboard displays to the roadway
Static Visual Acuity	Ability to see small details clearly	Reading distant traffic signs
Adaptation	Change in sensitivity to levels different of light	Adjust to changes in light upon entering a tunnel
Angular Movement	Seeing objects moving across the field of view	Judging the speed of cars crossing our paths
Movement in Depth	Detecting changes in visual image size	Judging the speed of an approaching vehicle
Color	Discrimination between different colors	Identifying the color of signals
Contrast Sensitivity	Seeing objects that are similar in brightness to their background	Detecting dark-clothed pedestrians at night
Depth Perception	Judgment of the distance of objects	Passing on two-lane roads with oncoming traffic
Dynamic Visual Acuity	Ability to see objects that are in motion relative to the eye	Reading traffic signs while moving
Eye Movement	Changing the direction of gaze	Scanning the road environment for hazards
Glare Sensitivity	Ability to resist and recover from the effects of glare	Reduction in visual performance due to headlight glare
Peripheral Vision	Detection of objects at the side of the visual field	Seeing a bicycle approaching from the left
Vergence	Angle between the eyes' line of sight	Change from looking at the dashboard to the road

(2) Fields of Vision

Figure 2.1 illustrates three distinct fields of vision, each of which is important to the driving task:

- acute or clear vision cone—3° to 10° around the line of sight; legend can be read only within this narrow field of vision;
- fairly clear vision cone— 10° to 12° around the line of sight; color and shape can be identified in this field;
- peripheral vision—this field may extend up to 90° to the right and left of the centerline of the pupil, and up to 60° above and 70° below the line of sight. Stationary objects are generally not seen in the peripheral vision field, but the movement of objects through this field is detected.

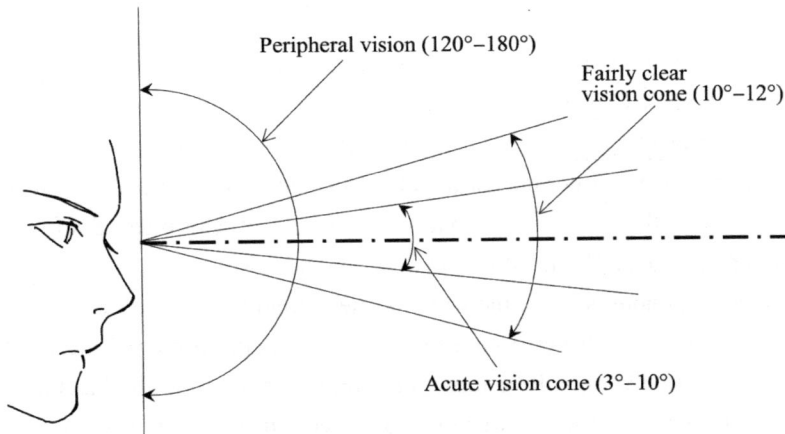

Peripheral vision (120°–180°)

Fairly clear vision cone (10°–12°)

Acute vision cone (3°–10°)

Figure 2.1   Illustration of Fields of Vision

These fields of vision, however, are defined for a stationary person. In particular, the peripheral vision field narrows, as speed increases, to as little as 100° at 32 km/h and to 40° at 96 km/h.

The driver's visual landscape is both complex and rapidly changing. Approaching objects appear to expand in size while other vehicles and stationary objects are in relative motion both to the driver and to each other. The typical driver essentially samples the available visual information and selects appropriate cues to make driving decisions.

The fields of vision affect a number of traffic engineering practices and functions. Traffic signs, for example, are placed so that they can be read within the acute vision field without requiring drivers to change their line of sight. Thus they are generally placed within a 10° range of the driver's expected line of sight, which is assumed to be in line with the highway alignment. This leads to signs that are intended to be read when they are a significant distance from the driver; in turn, this implies how large the sign and its lettering must be to be comprehended at that distance. Objects or other vehicles located in the fairly clear and peripheral vision fields may draw the driver's attention to an important event occurring in that field, such as the approach of a vehicle on an intersection street or driveway or a child running into the street after a ball. Once noticed, the driver may turn his or her head to examine the details of the situation.

Peripheral vision is the single most important factor when drivers estimate their speed. The movement of objects through the peripheral vision field is the driver's single most important indicator of speed. Old studies have demonstrated time and again that drivers deprived of peripheral vision (using blinders in experimental cases) and deprived of a working speedometer have little idea of how fast they are traveling.

(3) Important Visual Deficits

A number of visual problems can affect driver performance and behavior. Unless the condition causes a severe visual disability, drivers affected by various visual deficits often continue to drive.

Some of the more common problems involve cataracts (白内障), glaucoma (青光眼), peripheral vision deficits, ocular muscle imbalance (眼肌失衡), depth perception deficits (深度知觉缺陷), and color blindness (色盲). Drivers who have eye surgery to correct a problem may experience temporary or permanent impairments. Other diseases, such as diabetes (糖尿病), can have a significant negative impact on vision if not controlled. Some conditions, like cataracts and glaucoma, if untreated, can lead to blindness.

Although color blindness is not the worst of these conditions, it generally causes some difficulties for the affected driver because color is one of the principal means to impart information. Unfortunately, one of the most common forms of color blindness involves the inability to discern the difference between red and green. In the case of traffic signals, this could have a devastating (破坏性的) impact on the safety of such drivers. To ameliorate (改善) this difficulty to some degree, some blue pigment (蓝色素) has been added to green lights and some yellow pigment has been added to red lights, making them easier to discern by colorblind drivers. Also, the location of colors on signal heads has long been standardized, with red on the top and green on the bottom of vertical signal heads. On horizontal heads, red is on the left and green on the right. Arrow indications are either located on a separate signal head or placed below or to the right of ball indications on a mixed signal head.

2.1.2　Perception-Reaction Time

The second critical driver characteristic is ***perception-reaction time*** (***PRT***). During perception and reaction, the driver must perform four distinct processes.

- Detection. In this phase, an object or condition of concern enters the driver's field of vision, and the driver becomes consciously aware that something requiring a response is present.
- Identification. In this phase, the driver acquires sufficient information concerning the

object or condition to allow the consideration of an appropriate response.

- Decision. Once identification of the object or condition is sufficiently completed, the driver must analyze the information and make a decision about how to respond.
- Response. After a decision has been reached, the response is now physically implemented by the driver.

In some of the literature, the four phases of PRT are referred to as perception, identification, emotion, and volition, leading to the term *"PIEV time"*. This text uses PRT, but you should understand that it is equivalent to PIEV time.

(1) Design Values

Like all human characteristics, perception-reaction times vary widely among drivers, as do a variety of other factors, including the type and complexity of the event perceived and the environmental conditions at the time of the response.

Nevertheless, design values for various applications must be selected. The American Association of State Highway and Transportation Officials (AASHTO) mandates the use of 2.5 s for most computations involving braking reactions. This value is believed to be approximately a 90th percentile criterion (i.e., 90% of all drivers have a PRT as fast or faster than 2.5 s).

For signal timing purposes, the Institute of Transportation Engineers recommends a PRT time of 1.0 s. Because of the simplicity of the response and the preconditioning of drivers to respond to signals, the PRT time is significantly less than that for a braking response on an open highway. Although this is a lower value, it still represents an approximately 85th percentile for the particular situation of responding to a traffic signal.

AASHTO criteria, however, recognize that in certain more complex situations, drivers may need considerably more time to react than 1.0 or 2.5 s. Situations where drivers must detect and react to unexpected events, or a difficult-to-perceive information source in a cluttered highway environment, or a situation in which there is a likelihood of error involving either information reception, decisions, or actions all would result in increased PRT times. Some of the examples cited by AASHTO of locations where such situations might exist include complex interchanges and intersections where unusual movements are encountered and changes in highway cross sections such as toll plazas, lane drops, and areas where the roadway environment is cluttered with visual distractions. Where a collision avoidance maneuver is required, AASHTO criteria call for a PRT of 3.0 s for stops on rural roads and 9.1 s for stops on urban roads. Where collision avoidance requires speed, path, and/or direction changes, AASHTO recommends a PRT of between 10.2 and 11.2 s on rural roads, between 12.1 and 12.9 s on suburban roads, and between 14.0 and 14.5 s on urban roads.

(2) Expectancy

The concept of expectancy is important for the driving task and has a significant impact on the perception-reaction process and PRT. Simply put, drivers react more quickly to situations they expect to encounter as opposed to those that they do not expect to encounter. There are three different types of expectancies.

- Continuity. Experiences of the immediate past are generally expected to continue. Drivers do not, for example, expect the vehicle they are following to suddenly slow down.
- Event. Things that have not happened previously will not happen. If no vehicles have been observed entering the roadway from a small driveway over a reasonable period of time, then the driver will assume that none will enter now.
- Temporal. When events are cyclic, such as a traffic signal, the longer a given state is observed, drivers will assume that it is more likely a change will occur.

Given the obvious importance of expectancy on PRT, traffic engineers must strive to avoid designing "unexpected" events into roadway systems and traffic controls. If there are all right-hand ramps on a given freeway, for example, left-hand ramps should be avoided if at all possible. If absolutely required, guide signs must be very carefully designed to alert drivers to the existence and location of the left-hand ramp, so that when they reach it, it is no longer "unexpected".

(3) Other Factors Affecting PRT

In general, PRTs increase with a number of factors, including (a) age, (b) fatigue, (c) complexity of reaction, and (d) presence of alcohol and/or drugs in the drive's system. Although these trends are well documented, they are generally accounted for in recommended design values, with the exception of the impact of alcohol and drugs. The latter is addressed primarily through enforcement of ever-stricter driving while intoxicated/ driving under the influence (DWI/DUI) laws in the various states, with the intent of removing such drivers from the system, especially where repeated violations make them a significant safety risk. Some of the more general affects of alcohol and drugs, as well as aging, on driver characteristics are discussed in a later section.

(4) Reaction Distance

The most critical impact of perception-reaction time is the distance the vehicle travels while the driver goes through the process. In the example of a simple braking reaction, the PRT begins when the driver first becomes aware of an event or object in his or her field of vision and ends when his or her foot is applied to the brake. During this time, the vehicle continues along its original course at its initial speed. Only after the foot is applied to the brake pedal does the vehicle begin to slow down in response to the stimulus (刺激).

The reaction distance is simply the PRT multiplied by the initial speed of the vehicle. Because speed is generally in units of km/h and PRT is in units of seconds, it is convenient to convert speeds to m/s for use: 1 km/h = 0.278 m/s.

Thus, the reaction distance may be computed as:

$$d_r = 0.278 V_0 \cdot t \tag{2.1}$$

where

d_r— reaction distance, m;

V_0— initial speed of vehicle, km/h;

t— reaction time, s.

The importance of this factor is illustrated in the following sample problem. A driver rounds a curve at a speed of 100 km/h and sees a truck overturned on the roadway ahead. How far will the driver's vehicle travel before the driver's foot reaches the brake? Applying the AASHTO standard of 2.5 s for braking reactions:

$$d_r = 0.278 \cdot V_0 \cdot t = 0.278 \times 100 \times 2.5 = 69.5 \text{ m}$$

The vehicle will travel 69.5 m (approximately 11 to 12 car lengths) before the driver even engages the brake. The implication of this is frightening. If the overturned truck is closer to the vehicle than 69.5 m when noticed by the driver, not only will the driver hit the truck, he or she will do so at full speed—100 km/h. Deceleration begins only when the brake is engaged—after the perception-reaction process has been completed.

2.1.3   Pedestrian Characteristics

One of the most critical safety problems in any highway and street system involves the interactions of vehicles and pedestrians. A substantial number of traffic accidents and fatalities involve pedestrians. This is not surprising because in any contact between a pedestrian and a vehicle, the pedestrian is at a significant disadvantage.

Virtually all of the interactions between pedestrians and vehicles occur as pedestrians cross the street at intersections and at mid-block locations. At signalized intersections, safe accommodation of pedestrian crossings is as critical as vehicle requirements in establishing an appropriate timing pattern. Pedestrian walking speed in crosswalks is the most important factor in the consideration of pedestrians in signal timing.

At unsignalized crossing locations, gap-acceptance behavior of pedestrians is another important consideration. "Gap acceptance" refers to the clear time intervals between vehicles encroaching on the crossing path and the behavior of pedestrians in "accepting" them to cross through.

(1) Walking Characteristics

The basic parameters commonly used in pedestrian traffic are stride frequency, stride length and stride speed.

Stride frequency refers to the number of steps taken by a pedestrian in a unit of time. The unit is usually steps/min. The number of pedestrian steps per minute varies from 80 to 150, and the common value is 120.

Stride length, also known as step length, refers to the length of each step taken by a pedestrian when walking, and the unit is cm or m. The average stride length of Chinese pedestrians is about 63.7 cm. Men had a slightly larger stride length than women, and stride length e did not correlate with stride speed.

Stride speed is the distance traveled by the pedestrian in unit time, which is generally expressed as m/s, m/min or km/h. Stride speed is not only different for men and women, but also related to the characteristics of the walking path. The stride speed of 1-1.2 m/s is generally used in the design.

(2) *Gap Acceptance*

When a pedestrian crosses at an uncontrolled (either by signals, STOP, or YIELD signs) location, either at an intersection or at a mid-block location, the pedestrian must select an appropriate "gap" in the traffic stream through which to cross. The "gap" in traffic is measured as the time lag between two vehicles in any lane encroaching on the pedestrian's crossing path. As the pedestrian waits to cross, he or she views gaps and decides whether to "accept" or "reject" the gap for a safe crossing.

Gap acceptance behavior, however, is quite complex and varies with a number of other factors, including the speed of approaching vehicles, the width of the street, the frequency distribution of gaps in the traffic stream, waiting time, and others. Nevertheless, this is an important characteristic that must be considered due to its obvious safety implications.

2.1.4   Impacts of Drugs and Alcohol on Road Users

The effect of drugs and alcohol on drivers has received well-deserved national attention for many years, leading to substantial strengthening of DWI/DUI laws and enforcement. These factors remain, however, a significant contributor to traffic fatalities and accidents. And drivers are not the only road users who contribute to the nation's accident and fatality statistics. The World Health Organization's accident survey shows that about 50%-60% of traffic accidents are related to drunk driving. The relationship between a driver's blood alcohol level and accidents is shown in Table 2.2.

Table 2.2   Illustration of Relationships between Drivers' Blood Alcohol Level and Accidents

Blood Alcohol Level (‰)	Accidents (times)		
	Death	**Injured**	**Damage**
0	1	1	1
0.1	1.20	1.16	1.07
0.3	1.75	1.57	1.24

continued

Blood Alcohol Level (‰)	Accidents (times)		
	Death	Injured	Damage
0.5	2.53	2.12	1.43
0.7	3.67	2.87	1.65
0.9	5.32	3.87	1.90
1.1	7.71	5.23	2.19
1.3	11.18	7.07	2.52
1.5	16.21	9.55	2.91

The importance of these isolated statistics is to make the following point: legal limits for DWI/DUI do not define the point at which alcohol and/or drugs influence the road user. Recognizing this is important for individuals to ensure safe driving it is now causing many countries to reduce their legal limits on alcohol to 0.08%, and for some to consider "zero tolerance" criteria (0.01%) for new drivers for the first year or two after they are licensed.

Drugs and alcohol have effects on various driving factors, such as steering difficulties, disoriented and confused, driving faster, abrupt stopping and starting, distracted, and so on. Note that for many factors, impairment of driver function begins at levels well below the legal limits—for some factors at blood-alcohol levels as low as 0.05%. What all of these factors add up to is an impaired driver. This combination of impairments leads to longer PRT times, poor judgments, and actions that can and do cause accidents. Because few of these factors can be ameliorated (改善) by design or control (although good designs and well-designed controls help both impaired and unimpaired drivers), enforcement and education are critical elements in reducing the incidence of DWI/DUI and the accidents and deaths that result.

Studies also highlight the danger caused by pedestrians who are impaired by drugs or alcohol. In the case of impaired pedestrians, the danger is primarily to themselves. Nevertheless, if crossing a street or highway is required, "walking while impaired" is also quite dangerous. Again, enforcement and education are the major weapons in combating the problem because not a great deal can be done through design or control to address the issue.

Both motorists and pedestrians should also be aware of the impact of common prescription (处方药) and over-the-counter medications on their performance capabilities. Many legitimate medications have effects that are similar to those of alcohol and/or illegal drugs. Users of medications should always be aware of the side effects of what they use [a most frequent effect of many drugs is drowsiness (困倦)], and to exercise care and good judgment when considering whether or not to drive. Some legitimate drugs can have a direct impact on blood-alcohol levels and can render a motorist legally intoxicated without "drinking".

2.1.5   Impacts of Aging on Road Users

As life expectancy continues to rise, the number of older drivers has risen dramatically over the past several decades. Thus, it becomes increasingly important to understand how aging affects drivers' needs and limitations and how these should impact design and control decisions.

Many visual acuity factors deteriorate with age, including both static and dynamic visual acuity, glare sensitivity and recovery, night vision, and speed of eye movements. Such ailments as cataracts, glaucoma, macular degeneration, and diabetes are also more common as people age, and these conditions have negative impacts on vision.

The increasing prevalence of older drivers presents a number of problems for both traffic engineers and public officials. On one hand, at some point, deterioration of various capabilities inevitably leads to revocation of the right to drive. On the other hand, driving is the principal means of mobility and accessibility in most parts of the nation, and the alternatives for those who can no longer drive are either limited or expensive. The response to the issue of an aging driver population must have many components, including appropriate licensing standards, consideration of some license restrictions on older drivers (e.g., a daytime-only license), provision of efficient and affordable transportation alternatives, and increased consideration of their needs, particularly in the design and implementation of control devices and traffic regulations. Older drivers may be helped, for example, by such measures as larger lettering on signs, better highway lighting, larger and brighter signals, and other measures. Better education can serve to make older drivers more aware of the types of deficits they face and how best to deal with them. More frequent testing of key characteristics such as eyesight may help ensure that prescriptions for glasses and/or contact lenses are frequently updated.

2.1.6   Psychological, Personality, and Related Factors

Over the past decade, traffic engineers and the public in general have become acquainted with the term *road rage*. Commonly applied to drivers who lose control of themselves and react to a wide variety of situations violently, improperly, and almost always dangerously, the problem (which has always existed) is now getting well-deserved attention. Road rage, however, is a colloquial term, and is applied to everything from a direct physical assault by one road user on another to a variety of *aggressive driving behaviors*.

The following attitudes characterize aggressive drivers:
- the desire to get to one's destination as quickly as possible, leading to the expression of anger at other drivers/pedestrians who impede this desire;
- the need to compete with other fast cars;
- the need to respond competitively to other aggressive drivers;
- contempt for other drivers who do not drive, look, and act as they do on the road;

- the belief that it is their right to "hit back" at other drivers whose driving behavior threatens them.

Road rage is the extreme expression of a driver's psychological and personal displeasure over the traffic situation he or she has encountered. It does, however, remind traffic engineers that drivers display a wide range of behaviors in accordance with their own personalities and psychological characteristics.

Once again, most of these factors cannot be addressed directly through design or control decisions and are best treated through vigorous enforcement and educational programs.

2.2   Vehicles

According to the International Energy Agency (IEA), there were about 1.3 billion vehicles on the road by 2021. In 2022, approximately 319 million registered vehicles were in China, the world's largest number of motor vehicles.

Mastering vehicle characteristics plays an important role in completing a certain task of traffic engineering. The size of vehicles will affect the design of traffic facilities such as road alignment, headroom and parking lot. The characteristics of these vehicles vary as widely as those of the motorists who drive them, all of which will affect the characteristics of traffic flow and traffic safety.

2.2.1   Types of Vehicles

In the USA, motor vehicles are classified by AASHTO into four main categories:
- passenger cars—all passenger cars, SUVs, minivans, vans, and pickup trucks;
- buses—intercity motor coaches, transit buses, school buses, and articulated buses;
- trucks—single-unit trucks, tractor-trailer (牵引式挂车), and tractor-semi-trailer (牵引式半挂车) combination vehicles;
- recreational vehicles—motor homes, cars with various types of trailers (boat, campers, motorcycles, etc.).

In China, motor vehicles are classified by *Road Traffic Management—Types of Motor Vehicles* (GA 802—2019) into three main categories: passenger vehicles, trucks and special operation vehicles. The different vehicles are subdivided into mini, small, medium, large or heavy (Table 2.3, Table 2.4).

Table 2.3   Illustration of Classification and Specification of Passenger Vehicles

Classification	Specification
Large	Length of vehicles $\geq$ 6 m or passenger capacity $\geq$ 20 persons
Medium	Length of vehicles < 6 m and passenger capacity from 10 to 19 persons
Small	Length of vehicles < 6 m and passenger capacity $\leq$ 9 persons
Mini	Length of vehicles < 3.5 m and total displacement of engine cylinders $\leq$ 1,000 mL

Table 2.4   Illustration of Classification and Specification of Trucks

Classification	Specification
Heavy	Maximum allowable total mass $\geq$ 12,000 kg
Medium	Length of vehicles $\geq$ 6 m or maximum allowable total mass $\geq$ 4,500 kg and < 12,000 kg
Light	Length of vehicles < 6 m and maximum allowable total mass < 4,500 kg
Mini	Length of vehicles $\geq$ 3.5 m and maximum allowable total mass $\leq$ 1,800 kg
Three-wheeled Truck	Length of vehicles $\leq$ 4.6 m, width $\leq$ 1.6 m, height $\leq$ 2.0 m and maximum allowable total mass $\leq$ 2,000 kg with three wheels*
Low-speed Truck	Length of vehicles $\leq$ 6.0 m, width $\leq$ 2.0 m, height $\leq$ 2.5 m and maximum allowable total mass $\leq$ 4,500 kg with four wheels*

* More details can be found in *Road Traffic Management—Types of Motor Vehicles* (GA 802—2019).

Motorcycles and bicycles also use highway and street facilities but are not isolated as a separate category because their characteristics do not usually limit or define design or control needs. A number of critical vehicle properties must be accounted for in the design of roadways and traffic controls. These include:

- braking and deceleration;
- acceleration;
- low-speed turning characteristics;
- high-speed turning characteristics.

In more general terms, the issues associated with vehicles of vastly differing size, weight, and operating characteristics sharing roadways must also be addressed by traffic engineers.

2.2.2   Concept of the Design Vehicle

Given the immense range of vehicle types using street and highway facilities, it is necessary to adopt standard vehicle characteristics for design and control purposes. Design vehicles are primarily employed in the design of turning roadways and intersection curbs, and they are used to help determine appropriate lane widths and such specific design features as lane-widening on curves. Key to such usage, however, is the selection of an appropriate design vehicle for various types of facilities and situations. In general, the design should consider the largest vehicle likely to use the facility with a reasonable frequency.

In considering the selection of a design vehicle, it must be remembered that all parts of the street and highway network must be accessible to emergency vehicles, including fire engines, ambulances, emergency evacuation vehicles, and emergency repair vehicles, among others. Therefore the single-unit truck is usually the minimum design vehicle selected for most local street applications. The mobility of hook-and-ladder fire vehicles is enhanced by having rear-axle steering that allows these vehicles to negotiate sharper turns than would normally be possible for combination vehicles, so the use of a single-unit truck as a design vehicle for local streets is not considered to hinder emergency vehicles.

The passenger car is used as a design vehicle only in parking lots, and even there, access to emergency vehicles must be considered. For most other classes or types of highways and intersections, the selection of a design vehicle must consider the expected vehicle mix. In general, the design vehicle selected should easily accommodate 95% or more of the expected vehicle mix.

The physical dimensions of design vehicles are also important considerations. Design vehicle heights range from 1.3 m for a passenger car to 4.2 m for the largest trucks. Overhead clearances of overpass and sign structures, electrical wires, and other overhead appurtenances (附属物) should be sufficient to allow the largest anticipated vehicles to proceed. Because all facilities must accommodate a wide variety of potential emergency vehicles, use of 4.5 m for minimum clearances is advisable for most facilities.

The width of design vehicles ranges from 2.0 m for passenger cars to 2.5 m for the largest trucks (excluding special "wide load" vehicles such as a tractor pulling a prefabricated (定制的) or motor home). This should influence the design of such features as lane width and shoulders. For most facilities, it is desirable to use the standard 3.5 m lane width. Narrower lanes may be considered for some types of facilities when necessary, but given the width of modern vehicles, 2.8 m is a reasonable minimum for virtually all applications in China.

2.2.3   Turning Characteristics of Vehicles

There are two conditions under which vehicles must make turns:
- low-speed turns ($\leqslant 16$ km/h);

- high-speed turns (>16 km/h).

Low-speed turns are limited by the characteristics of the vehicle because the minimum radius allowed by the vehicle's steering mechanism can be supported at such speeds. AASHTO specifies minimum design radii for each of the design vehicles, based on the centerline turning radius and minimum inside turning radius of each vehicle. Although the actual turning radius of a vehicle is controlled by the front wheels, rear wheels do not follow the same path. Rear wheels "off-track" as they are dragged through the turning movement. Note that *the minimum turning radius* is defined by the track of the front outside wheel.

High-speed turns are limited by the dynamics of side friction between the roadway and the tires, and by the *superelevation* (cross-slope) of the roadway. When involved in a high-speed turn on a highway curve, centripetal forces of momentum are exerted on the vehicle to continue on a straight path. To hold the curve, these forces are opposed by side friction and superelevation. Superelevation is the cross-slope of the roadway, always with the lower edge in the direction of the curve. The sloped roadway provides an element of horizontal support for the vehicle. Side-friction forces represent the resistance to sliding provided across the plane of the surface between the vehicle's tires and the roadway.

Figure 2.2 shows the turning template of a motor vehicles. The relationship between the minimum design turning radius of the circular lane and the turning radius of a motor vehicle is presented in Equations 2.2 to 2.6. The minimum turning radius of motor vehicles is listed in Table 2.5.

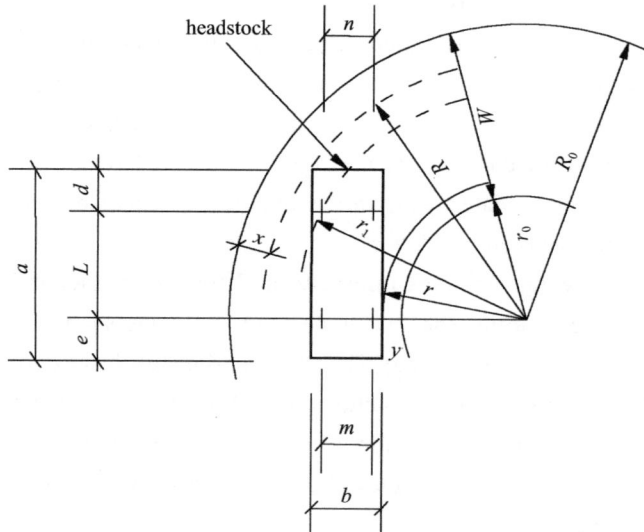

Figure 2.2   Illustration of Turning Template

$$W = R_0 - r_0 \qquad (2.2)$$

$$R_0 = R + x \qquad (2.3)$$

$$r_0 = r - y \tag{2.4}$$

$$R = \sqrt{(L+d)^2 + (r+b)^2} \tag{2.5}$$

$$r = \sqrt{r_1^2 - L^2} - \frac{b+n}{2} \tag{2.6}$$

where

a — the length of the vehicle;

b — the width of the vehicle;

d — front overhang dimension;

e — rear overhang dimension;

L — wheelbase;

m — rear track;

n — front track;

r_1 — the minimum turning radius;

R_0 — outer radius of the circular lane;

r_0 — inner radius of the circular lane;

R — circular outer radius of the vehicle;

r — circular inner radius of the vehicle;

W — minimum clear width of the circular lane;

x — the safety distance between the outermost point of the vehicle track and the outside of the circular lane;

y — the safety distance between the innermost point of the vehicle track and the inside of the circular lane.

Table 2.5　Illustration of the Minimum Turning Radius of Motor Vehicles

Classification	Minimum Turning Radius (m)
Large	9.00-10.50
Medium	7.20-9.00
Light	6.00-7.20
Small	6.00
Mini	4.50

2.2.4　Braking Characteristics

Another critical characteristic of vehicles is their ability to stop (or decelerate) once the brakes have been engaged. Again, basic physics relationships are used. The distance traveled during a stop is the average speed during the stop multiplied by the time taken to stop, or:

$$V_t = V_0 - at = 0 \Rightarrow t = \frac{V_0}{a} \qquad (2.7)$$

$$d_b = \bar{V} \cdot t = \left(\frac{V_0}{2}\right) \cdot \left(\frac{V_0}{a}\right) = \frac{V_0^2}{2a} \qquad (2.8)$$

where

d_b — braking distance, m;

V_0 — initial speed of vehicle, m/s;

a — deceleration rate, m/s^2.

It is often useful to express this equation in terms of *the **coefficient of forward rolling or skidding friction***, φ, where $a = \varphi \cdot g$, and g is the acceleration due to gravity, 9.8 m/s². Then:

$$d_b = \frac{V_0^2}{19.6\varphi} \qquad (2.9)$$

where

φ — coefficient of forward rolling or skidding friction.

When the effects of grade are considered, and where a braking cycle leading to a reduced speed other than "0" is considered, the equation becomes:

$$d_b = \frac{V_0^2 - V_t^2}{254(\varphi \pm i)} \qquad (2.10)$$

where

i — grade, %;

V_0 — initial speed, km/h;

V_t — final speed, km/h.

When there is an upgrade, a "+" is used; a "−" is used for downgrades. This results in shorter braking distances on upgrades, where gravity helps deceleration, and longer braking distances on downgrades, where gravity causes acceleration.

Consider the following case: Once the brakes are engaged, what distance is covered bringing a vehicle traveling at 60 km/h on a 3% downgrade to a complete stop (V_t= 0 km/h, φ=0.348). Applying Equation 2.10:

$$d_b = \frac{V_0^2 - V_t^2}{254(\varphi \pm i)} = \frac{60^2 - 0}{254 \times (0.348 - 0.03)} = 44.57 \text{ m}$$

The braking distance formula is also a favorite tool of accident investigators. It can be used to estimate the initial speed of a vehicle using measured skid marks and an estimated final speed based on damage assessments.

2.2.5 Acceleration Characteristics

The flip side of deceleration is acceleration. Passenger cars are able to accelerate at significantly higher rates than commercial vehicles. Acceleration is highest at low speeds and decreases with increasing speed. Consider the distance required for a car and a truck to accelerate to 40 km/h. Converting speed from km/h to m/s:

$$V_t = V_0 + at = 0 + at \Rightarrow t = \frac{V_t}{a} \tag{2.11}$$

$$d_a = \overline{V} \cdot t = \left(\frac{V_t}{2}\right) \cdot \left(\frac{V_t}{a}\right) = \frac{V_t^2}{2a} \tag{2.12}$$

where
d_a— acceleration distance, m;
V_0— initial speed, m/s;
V_t— final speed, m/s;
a— acceleration rate, m/s².

The disparity between passenger cars and trucks is significant. If a car is at a "red" signal behind a truck, the truck will significantly delay the car. If a truck is following a car in a standing queue, a large gap between the two will occur as they accelerate.

Unfortunately, not much can be done about this disparity in terms of design and control. In the analysis of highway capacity, however, the disparity between trucks and cars in terms of acceleration and in terms of their ability to sustain speeds on upgrades leads to the concept of "*passenger car equivalency*". Depending on the type of facility, severity and length of grade, and other factors, one truck may consume as much roadway capacity as six to seven or more passenger cars. Thus the disparity in key operating characteristics of trucks and passenger cars is taken into account in design by providing additional capacity as needed.

2.3 Total Stopping Distance and Applications

The total distance to bring a vehicle to a full stop, from the time the need to do so is first noted, is the sum of the reaction distance, d_r, and the braking distance, d_b. If Equation 2.1 (for d_r) and Equation 2.10 (for d_b) are combined, the total stopping distance becomes:

$$d = 0.278V_0 \cdot t + \frac{V_0^2 - V_t^2}{254(\varphi \pm i)} \tag{2.13}$$

where
d — total stopping distance, m;
V_0 — initial speed, km/h;

V_t — final speed, km/h;

t — reaction time, s;

i — grade, %.

The concept of total stopping distance is critical for many applications in traffic engineering. Three of the more important applications are discussed in the sections that follow.

2.3.1　Safe Stopping Sight Distance

One of the most fundamental principles of highway design is that the driver must be able to see far enough to avoid a potential hazard or collision. Thus, on all roadway sections, the driver must have a sight distance that is at least equivalent to the total stopping distance required at the design speed. We name it ***stopping sight distance***.

Essentially, this requirement addresses this critical concern: A driver rounding a horizontal curve and/or negotiating a vertical curve is confronted with a downed tree, an overturned truck, or some other situation that completely blocks the roadway. The only alternative for avoiding a collision is to stop. The design must be such that at every point along its length, the driver has a clear line of vision for at least one full stopping distance. By ensuring this, the driver can never be confronted with the need to stop without having sufficient distance to do so.

Consider a section of rural freeway with a design speed of 110 km/h. On a section of level terrain, what safe stopping distance must be provided? Equation 2.13 is used with a final speed (V_t) of "0"and the standard reaction time of 2.5 s. Then:

$$d = 0.278 \cdot V_0 \cdot t + \frac{V_0^2 - V_t^2}{254(\varphi \pm i)} = 0.278 \times 110 \times 2.5 + \frac{110^2 - 0^2}{254 \times (0.348 \pm 0)} = 213.34 \,\text{m}$$

This means that for the entire length of this roadway section, drivers must be able to see at least 213.34 m ahead. Providing this safe stopping sight distance will limit various elements of horizontal and vertical alignment.

What could happen, for example, if a section of this roadway provided a sight distance of only 150 m? It would now be possible that a driver would initially notice an obstruction when it is only 150 m away. If the driver were approaching at the designed speed of 110 km/h, a collision would occur. Again, assuming design values of reaction time and forward skidding friction, Equation 2.13 could be solved for the collision speed (i.e., the final speed of the deceleration cycle), using a known deceleration distance of 150 m:

$$150 = 0.278 \times 110 \times 2.5 + \frac{110^2 - V_t^2}{254 \times (0.348 \pm 0)} \Rightarrow V_t = 74.82 \,\text{km/h}$$

If the assumed conditions hold, a collision at 74.82 km/h would occur. Of course, if the weather was dry and the driver had faster reactions than the design value (remember, 90%

of drivers do), the collision might occur at a lower speed or be avoided altogether. The point is that such a collision could occur if the sight distance were restricted to 150 m.

2.3.2 Decision Sight Distance

Although every point and section of a highway must be designed to provide at least a safe stopping sight distance, some sections should provide greater sight distance to allow drivers to react to potentially more complex situations than a simple stop.

Sight distances based on these collision-avoidance decision reaction times are referred to as *decision sight distances*. AASHTO recommends that decision sight distance be provided at interchanges or intersection locations where unusual or unexpected maneuvers are required; changes in cross sections such as lane drops and additions, toll plazas, and intense- demand areas where there is substantial "visual noise" from competing information (e.g., control devices, advertising, roadway elements, etc.).

The decision sight distance is found by using Equation 2.13, replacing the standard 2.5 s reaction time for stopping maneuvers with the appropriate collision avoidance reaction time for the situation.

Consider the decision sight distance required for a freeway section with a 100 km/h design speed approaching a busy urban interchange with many competing information sources. The approach is on a 3% downgrade. For this case, AASHTO suggests a reaction time up to 14.5 s to allow for complex path and speed changes in response to conditions. The decision sight distance is still based on the assumption that a worst case would require a complete stop. Thus the decision sight distance would be:

$$d = 0.278 \cdot V_0 \cdot t + \frac{V_0^2 - V_t^2}{254(\varphi \pm i)} = 0.278 \times 100 \times 14.5 + \frac{100^2 - 0^2}{254 \times (0.348 - 0.03)} = 526.91 \, \text{m}$$

AASHTO criteria for decision sight distances do not assume a stop maneuver for the speed/path/direction changes required in the most complex situations. The criteria, which are shown in Table 2.6, replace the braking distance in these cases with maneuver distances consistent with maneuver times between 3.5 and 4.5 s. During the maneuver time, the initial speed is assumed to be in effect. Thus for maneuvers involving speed, path, or direction change on rural, suburban, or urban roads, Equation 2.14 is used to find the decision sight distance.

$$d = 0.278 V_0 \cdot (t_r + t_m) \tag{2.14}$$

where

t_r — reaction time for appropriate avoidance maneuver, s;

t_m — maneuver time, s.

Table 2.6   Decision Sight Distances Resulting

Design Speed (km/h)	Assumed Maneuver Time (s)	Decision Sight Distance for Avoidance Maneuver (m)				
		A	B	C	D	E
		Equation 2.13		Equation 2.14		
Reaction Time (s)		3	9.1	11.2	12.9	14.5
40	4.5	53	121	175	193	211
60	4.5	95	196	262	290	317
80	4.0	146	282	338	376	411
100	4.0	207	377	423	470	514
110	3.5	242	428	450	502	550
120	3.5	278	482	490	547	600

Note: A: stop on a rural road; B: stop on an urban road; C: speed/path/direction change on a rural road; D: speed/path/direction change on a suburban road; E: speed/path/direction change on an urban road.

Thus in the sample problem posed previously, AASHTO would not assume a stop is required. At 100 km/h, a maneuver time of 4.0 s is used with the 14.5 s reaction time, and:

$$d = 0.278 \cdot V_0 \cdot (t_r + t_m) = 0.278 \times 100 \times (14.5 + 4.0) = 514.3 \text{ m}$$

The criteria for decision sight distance shown in Table 2.6 are developed from Equations 2.13 and 2.14 for the decision reaction times indicated for the five defined avoidance maneuvers.

Exercises

1. What are the steps included in the reaction time of drivers?
2. What are the static and dynamic visual acuities? Do they have any relationship?
3. Why do we have to determine the standard vehicles?
4. A driver takes 3.5 s to react to a complex situation while traveling at a speed of 60 km/h. How far does the vehicle travel before the driver initiates a physical response to the situation (i.e., putting his or her foot on the brake)?
5. A driver traveling at 80 km/h rounds a curve on a level grade to see a truck overturned across the roadway at a distance of 105 m. If the driver is able to decelerate at a rate of 3 m/s², at what speed will the vehicle hit the truck? Plot

the result for reaction times ranging from 0.50 to 5.00 s in increments of 0.5 s. Comment on the results.

6. A car hits a tree at an estimated speed of 40 km/h on a 3% upgrade. If skid marks of 37 m are observed on dry pavement ($\varphi=0.35$) followed by 76 m ($\varphi=0.25$) on a grass-stabilized shoulder, estimate the initial speed of the vehicle just before the pavement skid began.

7. Drivers must slow down from 100 km/h to 60 km/h to negotiate a severe curve on a rural highway. A warning sign for the curve is clearly visible for a distance of 40 m. How far in advance of the curve must the sign be located to ensure that vehicles have sufficient distance to decelerate safely? Use the standard reaction time and deceleration rate recommended by AASHTO for basic braking maneuvers.

8. What is the safe stopping distance for a section of rural freeway with a design speed of 120 km/h on a 3% downgrade?

Glossary

1. *Static visual acuity*: 静视力，待检人员站在视力图表前面，距视力表5 m，依次辨认视标测定的视力。

2. *Perception-reaction time (PRT)*: 感知–反应时间，驾驶员感知信号，经过辨认、判断、采取动作并使动作发生效果所需要的时间。该过程涵盖感知、判断决策和操纵三个阶段。

3. *PIEV time*: 同PRT，该过程可细分为感知、判断、情感（决策）和行动四个阶段。

4. *Stride frequency*: 步频，行人行走时在单位时间内跨步的次数，常用单位为步数/min。

5. *Stride length*: 步幅，又称步长，指行人行走时每跨出一步的长度，单位为cm或m。

6. *Stride speed*: 步速为行人在单位时间内所行进的距离，一般采用m/s、m/min或者km/h表示。

7. *Gap acceptance*: 可穿越间隙，指次要道路上车辆穿越主要道路车流所需的时间，或行人过街时穿越车流所需的时间。

8. *Road rage*: 路怒，指驾驶人带着愤怒的心情，或故意用不安全的方式驾驶车辆，此时驾驶人的驾驶行为具有攻击性，也可能单纯表现为情绪烦躁。

9. *Aggressive driving behaviors*: 攻击性驾驶行为，一种危害或倾向危害人身财产安全的驾车方式。具体表现为超速驾驶、追尾、从右侧超车、闯红灯、大声鸣笛、使用侮辱性手势、辱骂其他人、暴力行为等。

10. *The minimum turning radius*: 机动车最小转弯半径，机动车回转时，当转向盘转到极限位置，机动车以最低稳定车速转向行驶时，外侧转向轮的中心平面在支承平面上滚过的轨迹圆半径，表示机动车能够通过狭窄弯曲地带或绕过不可越过的障碍物的能力。

11. *Superelevation*: 弯道超高，为平衡机动车在弯道上行驶所产生的离心力所设置的弯道横向坡度而形成的高差。

12. *Coefficient of forward rolling or skidding friction*: 滑动摩擦系数，一个无量纲的比例因数，其值与两接触面的材料及表面状况（如粗糙度、干湿度、温度等）有关，大小由实验确定并载于工程手册。

13. *Passenger car equivalency*: 当量交通量，将总交通量中各类车辆交通量折算成标准车型交通量之和。

14. *Stopping sight distance*: 停车视距，指车辆以一定的速度行驶中，驾驶员自看到前方障碍物时起，至达到障碍物前安全停车止所需要的最短行驶距离。

15. *Decision sight distance*: 决策视距，驾驶员发现不可预知或潜在的危险并完成安全操作的距离。

Key Points

1. Briefly describe the visual characteristics of drivers.
   简述机动车驾驶员的视觉特性。
2. Briefly describe the reaction characteristics of drivers.
   简述机动车驾驶员的反应特性。
3. Briefly describe the traffic characteristics of pedestrians.
   简述行人交通特性。
4. Briefly describe the influencing factors of road users, including drugs, alcohol, age, psychology, personal attributes, etc.
   简述道路用户的影响因素，包括药物、酒精、年龄、心理、个人属性等。
5. Briefly describe the basic characteristics of vehicles.
   简述车辆的基本特性。
6. Briefly describe the stopping sight distance and its application.
   简述停车视距及其应用。

Chapter 3

Traffic Stream Characteristics

Traffic streams are made up of individual drivers and vehicles interacting with each other and with the physical elements of the roadway and its general environment. Because both driver behavior and vehicle characteristics vary, individual vehicles within the traffic stream do not behave in exactly the same manners. Further, no two traffic streams will behave in exactly the same way, even in similar circumstances, because driver behavior varies with local characteristics and driving habits.

In describing traffic streams in quantitative terms, the purpose is to both understand the inherent (固有的) variability in their characteristics and to define normal ranges of behavior. To do so, key parameters must be defined and measured. Traffic engineers will analyze, evaluate, and ultimately plan improvements in traffic facilities based on such parameters and their knowledge of normal ranges of behavior.

Traffic stream parameters fall into two broad categories. Macroscopic parameters describe the traffic stream as a whole; microscopic parameters describe the behavior of individual vehicles or pairs of vehicles within the traffic stream. The three principal macroscopic parameters that describe a traffic stream are (a) *volume* or *rate of flow*, (b) *speed*, and (c) *density*. Microscopic parameters include (a) the speed of individual vehicles, (b) *headway*, and (c) *spacing* (Figure 3.1).

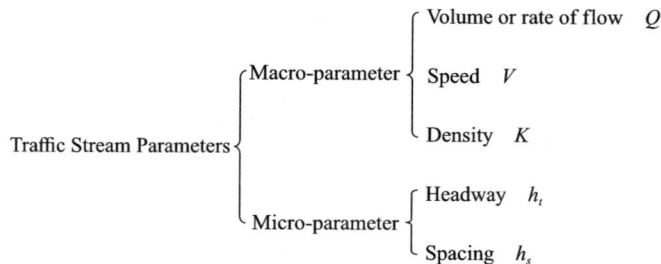

Traffic Stream Parameters
- Macro-parameter
  - Volume or rate of flow Q
  - Speed V
  - Density K
- Micro-parameter
  - Headway h_t
  - Spacing h_s

Figure 3.1 Parameters of Traffic Stream

3.1 Types of Facilities

Traffic flow is broadly separated into two principal categories, uninterrupted flow and interrupted flow.

Uninterrupted flow facilities have no external interruptions to the traffic stream. Pure uninterrupted flow exists primarily on freeways, where there are no intersections at grade, traffic signals, *STOP* or *YIELD signs*, or other interruptions external to the traffic stream itself. Because such facilities have full control of access, there are no intersections at grade, driveways, or any forms of direct access to abutting lands. Thus, the characteristics of the traffic stream are based solely on the interactions among vehicles and with the roadway and the general environment.

While pure uninterrupted flow exists only on freeways, it can also exist on sections of surface highway, most often in rural areas, where there are long distances between fixed interruptions. Thus, uninterrupted flow may exist on some sections of rural two-lane highways and rural and suburban multilane highways. As a very general guideline, it is believed that uninterrupted flow can exist in situations where the distance between traffic signals and/or other significant fixed interruptions is more than two miles.

It should be remembered that the term "uninterrupted flow" refers to a type of facility, not the quality of operations on that facility. Thus, a freeway that experiences breakdowns and long delays during peak hours is still operating under uninterrupted flow. The causes for the breakdowns and delay are not external to the traffic stream but are caused entirely by the internal interactions within the traffic stream.

Interrupted flow facilities are those that incorporate fixed external interruptions into their design and operation. The most frequent and operationally significant external interruption is the traffic signal. The traffic signal alternatively starts and stops a given traffic stream, creating a platoon. The traffic signal alternatively starts and stops a given traffic stream, creating a platoon of vehicles (车队) progressing down the facility. Other fixed interruptions include STOP and YIELD signs, unsignalized at-grade intersections, driveways, curb parking maneuvers (机动动作), and other land–access operations. Virtually all urban surface streets and highways are interrupted flow facilities.

The major difference between uninterrupted and interrupted flow facilities is the impact of time. On uninterrupted facilities, the physical facility is available to drivers and vehicles at all times. On a given interrupted flow facility, movement is periodically (周期性地) barred by a "red" signal. The signal timing, therefore, limits access to particular segments of the facility in time. Further, rather than a continuously moving traffic stream, at traffic signals, the traffic stream periodically stops and starts again. Interrupted flow is, therefore, more complex than uninterrupted flow.

3.2   Volume and Rate of Flow

Traffic volume is defined as the number of vehicles passing a point on a highway, or a given lane or direction of a highway, during a specified time interval. The unit of measurement for volume is simply "vehicles", although it is often expressed as "vehicles per unit time". Units of time used most often are "per day" or "per hour".

Daily volumes are used to establish trends over time, and for general planning purposes. Detailed design or control decisions require knowledge of hourly volumes for the peak hour(s) of the day.

Rates of flow are generally stated in units of "vehicles per hour", but represent flows that exist for periods of time less than one hour. A volume of 200 vehicles observed over a 15-minute period may be expressed as a rate of 200×4=800 vehicles/hour, even though 800 vehicles would not be observed if the full hour was counted. The 800 vehicles/h becomes a rate of flow that exists for a 15-minute interval.

3.2.1 Daily Volumes

As noted, daily volumes are used to document annual trends in highway usage. Forecasts based on observed trends can be used to help plan improved or new facilities to accommodate increasing demand. Four daily volume parameters that are widely used in traffic engineering:

- *AADT* (*Average Annual Daily Traffic*). The average 24-hour volume at a given location over a full 365-day year; the number of vehicles passing a site in a year divided by 365 days (366 days in a leap year).
- *AAWT* (*Average Annual Weekday Traffic*). The average 24-hour volume occurring on weekdays over a full 365-day year; the number of vehicles passing a site on weekdays in a year divided by the number of weekdays (usually 260 days).
- *ADT* (*Average Daily Traffic*). The average 24-hour volume at a given location over a defined time period of less than one year; a common application is to measure the ADT for each month of the year.
- *AWT* (*Average Weekday Traffic*). The average 24-hour weekday volume at a given location over a defined time period of less than one year; a common application is to measure the AWT for each month of the year.

All of these volumes are stated in terms of vehicles per day (vehs/day). Daily volumes are generally not differentiated by direction or lane but are totals for an entire facility at the designated location.

$$ADT = \frac{1}{n}\sum_{i=1}^{n} Q_i \tag{3.1}$$

where
Q_i — the daily volume of the i-th day, veh/d;
n — the number of days during the defined time period, d.

Table 3.1 illustrates the compilation of these daily volumes based on one year of count data at a sample location.

Table 3.1 Illustration of Daily Volume Parameters

1. Month	2. Number of Weekdays in a Month (days)	3. Total Days in a Month (days)	4. Total Monthly Volume (vehs)	5. Total Weekday Volume (vehs)	6. AWT 5/2 (vehs/day)	7. ADT 4/3 (vehs/day)
Jan.	22	31	425,000	208,000	9,455	13,710
Feb.	20	28	410,000	220,000	11,000	14,643

continued

1. Month	2. Number of Weekdays in a Month (days)	3. Total Days in a Month (days)	4. Total Monthly Volume (vehs)	5. Total Weekday Volume (vehs)	6. AWT 5/2 (vehs/day)	7. ADT 4/3 (vehs/day)
Mar.	22	31	385,000	185,000	8,409	12,419
Apr.	22	30	400,000	200,000	9,091	13,333
May	21	31	450,000	215,000	10,238	14,516
Jun.	22	30	500,000	230,000	10,455	16,667
Jul.	23	31	580,000	260,000	11,304	18,710
Aug.	21	31	570,000	260,000	12,381	18,387
Sep.	22	30	490,000	205,000	9,318	16,333
Oct.	22	31	420,000	190,000	8,636	13,548
Nov.	21	30	415,000	200,000	9,524	13,833
Dec.	22	31	400,000	210,000	9,545	12,903
Total	260	365	5,445,000	2,583,000	—	—

$AADT = 5,445,000 / 365 = 14,918$ vehs/d

$AAWT = 2,583,000 / 260 = 9,935$ vehs/d

3.2.2 Hourly Volumes

Daily volumes, although useful for planning purposes, cannot be used alone for design or operational analysis purposes. Volume varies considerably over the 24 hours of the day, with periods of maximum flow occurring during the morning and evening commuter "rush hours". The single hour of the day that has the highest hourly volume is referred to as the peak hour. The traffic volume within this hour is of greatest interest to traffic engineers for design and operational analysis. *The peak-hour volume* is generally stated as a directional volume (i.e., each direction of flow is counted separately).

Highways and controls must be designed to adequately serve the peak-hour traffic volume in the peak direction of flow. Because traffic going one way during the morning peak is going the opposite way during the evening peak, both sides of a facility must generally be designed to accommodate the peak directional flow during the peak hour. Where the directional disparity is significant, the concept of *reversible lanes* is sometimes useful. Washington DC, for example, makes extensive use of reversible lanes (direction changes by time of day) on its many wide boulevards (林荫大道) and some of its freeways.

In design, peak-hour volumes are sometimes estimated from projections of the AADT. Traffic forecasts are most often cast in terms of AADTs based on documented trends and/or forecasting models. Because daily volumes, such as the AADT, are more stable than hourly volumes, projections can be more confidently made using them. AADTs are converted to a peak-hour volume in the peak direction of flow. This is referred to as the "***directional design hour volume***" (***DDHV***, veh/h) and is found using the following relationship:

$$DDHV = AADT \times K_t \times K_D \qquad (3.2)$$

where

K_t— proportion of daily traffic occurring during the peak hour (设计小时系数);

K_D— proportion of peak hour traffic traveling in the peak direction of flow (方向分布系数).

For design, the K factor often represents the proportion of AADT occurring during the 30th peak hour of the year. If the 365 peak-hour volumes of the year at a given location are listed in descending order, the 30th peak hour is 30th on the list and represents a volume that is exceeded in only 29 hours or the year. For rural facilities, the 30th peak hour may have a significantly lower volume than the worst hour of the year, because critical peaks may occur only infrequently. In such cases, it is not considered economically feasible to invest large amounts of capital in providing additional capacity that will be used in only 29 hours of the year. In urban case, where traffic is frequently at capacity levels during all daily commuter peaks, the 30th peak hour is often not substantially different from the highest peak hour of the year.

3.2.3   Subhourly Volumes and Rates of Flow

Although hourly traffic volumes form the basis for many forms of traffic design and analysis, the variation of traffic within a given hour is also of considerable interest. The quality of traffic flow is often related to short-term fluctuations in traffic demand. A facility may have sufficient capacity to serve the peak-hour demand, but short-term peaks of flow within the hour may exceed capacity and create a breakdown.

Volumes observed for periods of less than one hour are generally expressed as equivalent hourly rates of flow. For example, 1,000 vehicles counted over a 15-minute interval could be expressed as 1,000 vehs/0.25 h = 4,000 vehs/h. The rate of flow of 4,000 vehs/h is valid for the 15-minute period in which the volume of 1,000 vehicles was observed. Table 3.2 illustrates the difference between volumes and rates of flow.

Table 3.2   Illustration of Volumes and Rates of Flow

Time Interval	Volume for Time Interval (vehs)	Rate of Flow for Time Interval (vehs/h)
5:00 − 5:15 pm	1,000	1,000/0.25=4,000
5:15 − 5:30 pm	1,100	1,100/0.25=4,400
5:30 − 5:45 pm	1,200	1,200/0.25=4,800
5:45 − 6:00 pm	900	900/0.25=3,600
5:00 − 6:00 pm	4,200	

The full hourly volume is the sum of the four 15-minute volume observations, or 4,200 vehs/h. The rate of flow for each 15-minute interval is the volume observed for that interval divided by 0.25 hour over which it was observed. In the worst period of time, 5:30 to 5:45 pm, the rate of flow is 4,800 vehs/h. This is a flow rate, not a volume. The actual volume for the hour is only 4,200 vehs/h.

Consider the situation that would exist if the capacity of the location in question were exactly 4,200 vehs/h. Although this is sufficient to handle the full-hour demand indicated in Table 2.2, the demand rate of flow during two of the 15-minute periods noted (5:15 to 5:30 pm and 5:30 to 5:45 pm) exceeds the capacity. The problem is that although demand may vary within a given hour, capacity is constant. In each 15-minute period, the capacity is 4,200/4 or 1,050 vehs. Thus, within the peak hour shown, queues will develop in the half-hour period between 5:15 and 5:45 pm, during which the demand exceeds the capacity.

The relationship between the hourly volume and the maximum rate of flow within the hour is defined by the *peak-hour factor* (*PHF*), as follows:

$$PHF_t = \frac{q}{V_{t-max} \times \frac{60}{t}} \tag{3.3}$$

where

PHF_t— the peak-hour factor with t-minute interval;

q— hourly volume, veh/h;

V_{t-max}— the maximum volume with t-minute interval, veh/ t-mins.

For the illustrative data in Table 3.2:

$$PHF_{15} = \frac{q}{V_{15-max} \times \frac{60}{15}} = \frac{4,200}{1,200 \times 4} = 0.875$$

The maximum possible value for the *PHF* is 1.00, which occurs when the volume in each interval is constant. For 15-minute periods, each would have a volume of exactly a quarter of the full hour volume. This indicates a condition in which there is virtually no variation of flow within the hour. The minimum value occurs when the entire hourly volume occurs in a single 15-minute interval. In this case, the PHF becomes 0.25 and represents the most extreme case of volume variation within the hour. In practical terms, the PHF generally varies between a low of 0.70 for rural and sparsely (贫乏地) developed areas to 0.98 in dense urban areas.

3.3   Speed and Travel Time

Speed is the second macroscopic parameter describing the state of a traffic stream. It is defined as a rate of motion in distance per unit time. Travel time is the time taken to traverse a defined section of roadway. Speed and travel time are inversely related:

$$V = \frac{L}{t}$$

(3.4)

where

V— speed, km/h or m/s;

L— distance traversed, km or m;

t— time to traverse distance, d, h, or s.

In a moving traffic stream, each vehicle travels at a different speed. Thus, the traffic stream does not have a single characteristic value, but rather a distribution of individual speeds. The traffic stream, taken as a whole, can be characterized by an average or typical speed.

There are two ways in which the average speed of a traffic stream can be computed:

- *time mean speed* (*TMS*). The average speed of all vehicles passing a point on a highway or lane over some specified time period;
- *space mean speed* (*SMS*). The average speed of all vehicles occupying a given section of highway or lane over some specified time period.

In essence, time mean speed is a point measure, while space mean speed describes a length of highway or lane. Figure 3.2 shows an example illustrating the differences between the two average speed measures.

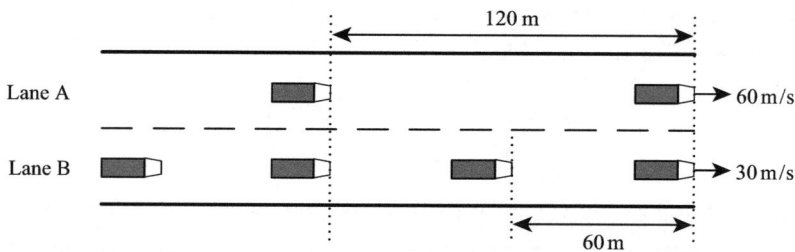

Figure 3.2   Space Mean and Time Mean Speed Illustrated

To measure time mean speed, an observer would stand by the side of the road and record the speed of each vehicle as it passes. Given the speeds and the spacing shown in Figure 3.2, a vehicle will pass the observer in Lane A every 120/60=2.0 s. Similarly, a vehicle will pass the observer in Lane B every 60/30=2.0 s. Thus, as long as the traffic stream maintains the conditions shown, for every n vehicles travelling at 60 m/s, the observer will also observe n vehicles travelling at 30 m/s. The *TMS* may then be computed as:

$$TMS = \frac{60n + 30n}{2n} = 45 \, \text{m/s}$$

To measure space mean speed (SMS), an observer would need an elevated location from which the full extent of the section may be viewed. Again, however, as long as the traffic stream remains stable and uniform, as shown, there will be twice as many vehicles in

Lane B as there are in Lane A. Therefore, the *SMS* is computed as:

$$SMS = \frac{60n + 30 \times 2n}{3n} = 40 \text{ m / s}$$

In effect, space mean speed accounts for the fact that it takes a vehicle travelling at 30 m/s twice as long to traverse the defined section as it does a vehicle travelling at 60 m/s. The space mean speed weights slower vehicles more heavily, based on the amount of time they occupy a highway section. Thus, the space mean speed is usually lower than the corresponding time mean speed, in which each vehicle is weighted equally. The two speed measures may conceivably be equal if all vehicles in the section are travelling at exactly the same speed.

Both the time mean speed and space mean speed may be computed from a series of measured travel times over a specified distance using the following relationships:

$$\overline{V}_t = \frac{1}{n}\sum_{i=1}^{n}\frac{L}{t_i} = \frac{1}{n}\sum_{i=1}^{n}V_i \tag{3.5}$$

$$\overline{V}_s = \frac{L}{\left(\sum_{i=1}^{n}t_i \big/ n\right)} = \frac{L \cdot n}{\sum_{i=1}^{n}t_i} = \frac{1}{\frac{1}{n}\sum_{i=1}^{n}\frac{1}{V_i}} \tag{3.6}$$

where

$\overline{V}_t$ — time mean speed, m/s;

$\overline{V}_s$ — space mean speed, m/s;

L — distance traversed, m;

n — number of observed vehicles;

t_i — time for vehicle "i" to traverse the section, s;

V_i — speed for vehicle "i", m/s.

TMS is computed by finding each individual vehicle's speed and taking a simple average of the results. *SMS* is computed by finding the average travel time for a vehicle to traverse the section and using the average travel time to compute a speed. Table 3.3 shows a sample problem in the computation of time mean and space mean speeds.

Table 3.3 Illustration Computation of *TMS* and *SMS*

Vehicle No.	Distance L (m)	Travel Time t (s)	Speed V (m/s)
1	300	17.0	300/17.0=17.6
2	300	20.0	300/20.0=15.0
3	300	23.0	300/23.0=13.0
4	300	25.0	300/25.0=12.0
5	300	24.0	300/24.0=12.5
6	300	20.0	300/20.0=15.0
Total	1,800	129	85.1
Average	1,800/6=300	129/6=21.5	85.1/6=14.2

$$\overline{V}_t = 14.2\, \text{m/s}$$

$$\overline{V}_s = \frac{300}{21.5} = 13.95\, \text{m/s}$$

3.4   Density and Occupancy

Density, the third primary measure of traffic stream characteristics, is defined as the number of vehicles occupying a given length of highway or lane, generally expressed as vehicle per kilometer or vehicles per kilometer per lane. It is considered the most important parameter of the three traffic stream elements, because it is the measure most directly related to traffic demand. Density is also an important measure of the quality of the traffic stream, as it is a measure of the proximity of other vehicles, a factor which influences freedom to maneuver and the psychological comfort of drivers.

$$K = \frac{N}{L} \tag{3.7}$$

where

K — density, veh/km/ln;

N — the number of vehicles, veh;

L — the length of observed road, km.

Density is difficult to measure directly, as an elevated vantage point from which the highway section under study may be observed is required. It is often computed from speed and flow rate measurements.

While density is difficult to measure directly, modern detectors can measure occupancy, which is a related parameter. *Occupancy* is defined as the proportion of time that a detector is "occupied", or covered, by a vehicle in a defined time period, as Figure 3.3 illustrates.

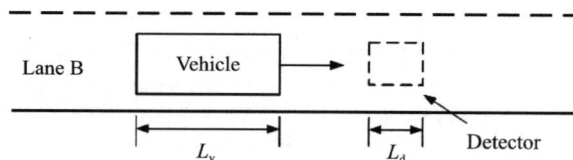

Figure 3.3   Occupancy Over a Detector

If "occupancy" over a given detector is "O", then density may be computed as:

$$K = \frac{1{,}000 \cdot O}{L_v + L_d} \tag{3.8}$$

where

K — density, veh/km/ln;

O — occupancy of the detector, %;

L_v — the average length of a vehicle, m;

L_d — the length of the detector (which is normally a magnetic loop detector), m.

Consider a case in which a detector records an occupancy of 0.2 for a 15-minute analysis period. If the average length of a vehicle is 8 m, and the detector is 1 m long, what is the density?

$$K = \frac{1,000 \times 0.2}{8+1} = 22.22 \text{ veh / km / ln}$$

The occupancy is measured by a specific detector in a specific lane. Thus, the density estimated from occupancy is in units of vehicles per kilometer per lane. If there are adjacent detectors in additional lanes, the density in each lane may be summed to provide a density in veh/km for a given direction of flow over several lanes.

3.5   Spacing and Headway: Microscopic Parameters

While flow, speed, and density represent macroscopic descriptors for the entire traffic stream, they can be related to microscopic parameters that describe individual vehicles within the traffic stream, or specific pairs of vehicles within the traffic stream.

Spacing is defined as the distance between successive vehicles in a traffic lane, measured from some common reference point on the vehicles, such as the front bumper or front wheels. The average spacing in a traffic lane can be directly related to the density of the lane:

$$K = \frac{1,000}{\overline{h}_s} \tag{3.9}$$

where

K — density, veh/km/ln;

$\overline{h}_s$ — average spacing between vehicles in the lane (平均车头间距), m.

Headway is defined as the time interval between successive vehicles as they pass a point along the lane, also measured between common reference points on the vehicles. The average headway in a lane is directly related to the rate of flow:

$$Q = \frac{3,600}{\overline{h}_t} \tag{3.10}$$

where

Q — rate of flow, veh/h/ln;

$\overline{h}_t$ — average headway in the lane (平均车头时距), s.

Microscopic measures are useful for many traffic analysis purposes. Because a spacing and/or a headway may be obtained for every pair of vehicles, the amount of data that can be collected in a short period of time is relatively large. A traffic stream with a volume of 1,000 vehs over a 15-minute time period results in a single value of rate of flow, space mean speed, and density when observed. There would be, however, 1,000 headway and spacing measurements, assuming that all vehicle pairs were observed.

Use of microscopic measures also allows various vehicle types to be isolated in the traffic scream. Passenger car flows and densities, for example, could be derived from isolating spacing and headway for pairs of passenger cars following each other. Heavy vehicles could be similarly isolated and studied for their specific characteristics.

Average speed can also be computed from headway and spacing measurements as:

$$\overline{V} = \overline{h_s} / \overline{h_t} \tag{3.11}$$

where

$\overline{V}$ — average speed, m/s;

$\overline{h_s}$ — average spacing between vehicles in the lane, m;

$\overline{h_t}$ — average headway in the lane, m.

A sample problem: traffic in a congested multilane highway lane is observed to have an average spacing of 61 m, and an average headway of 3.8 s. Estimate the rate of flow, density and speed of traffic in this lane.

Solution:

$$Q = \frac{3,600}{\overline{h_t}} = \frac{3,600}{3.8} = 947.37 \text{ veh / h / ln}$$

$$K = \frac{1,000}{\overline{h_s}} = \frac{1,000}{61} = 16.39 \text{ veh / km / ln}$$

$$\overline{V} = \overline{h_s} / \overline{h_t} = \frac{61}{3.8} = 16.05 \text{ m / s} = 57.78 \text{ km / h}$$

3.6　Relationships among Various Parameters

3.6.1　Relationship among Volume, Speed and Density

The three macroscopic measures of the state of a given traffic stream—flow, speed, and density—are related as follows:

$$Q = V \times K \tag{3.12}$$

where

Q — rate of flow, veh/h or veh/h/ln;

V — space mean speed, km/h;

K — density, veh/km or veh/km/ln.

Space mean speed and density are measures that refer to a specific section of a lane or highway, while flow rate is a point measure. The space mean speed and density measures must apply to the same defined section of roadway. Under stable flow condition (i.e., the flows entering and leaving the section are the same; no queues are forming within the section), the rate of flow computed by Equation 3.12 applies to any point within the section. Where unstable operations exist (a queue is forming within the section), the computed flow rate represents an average for all points within the section.

If a freeway lane was observed to have a space mean speed of 88 km/h and a density of 15.6 veh/km/ln, the flow rate in the lane could be estimated as:

$$Q = V \times K = 88 \times 1.6 = 140.8 \text{ veh} / \text{h} / \text{ln}$$

As noted previously, this relationship is most often used to estimate density, which is difficult to measure directly, from measured values of flow rate and space mean speed. Consider a freeway lane with a measured space mean speed of 96 km/h and a flow rate of 1,000 veh/h/ln. The density could be estimated from Equation 3.12 as:

$$K = \frac{Q}{V} = \frac{1,000}{96} = 10.42 \text{ veh} / \text{km} / \text{ln}$$

Equation 3.12 suggests that a given rate of flow (Q) could be achieved by an infinite number of speed (V) and density (K) pairs having the same product. Thankfully, this is not what happens, as it would make the mathematical interpretation of traffic flow unintelligible. There are additional relationships between pairs of these variables that restrict the number of combinations that can and do occur in the field.

The general form of these relationships is illustrated in Figure3.4. The exact shape and calibration of these relationships depends upon prevailing conditions, which vary from location to location and even over time at the same location.

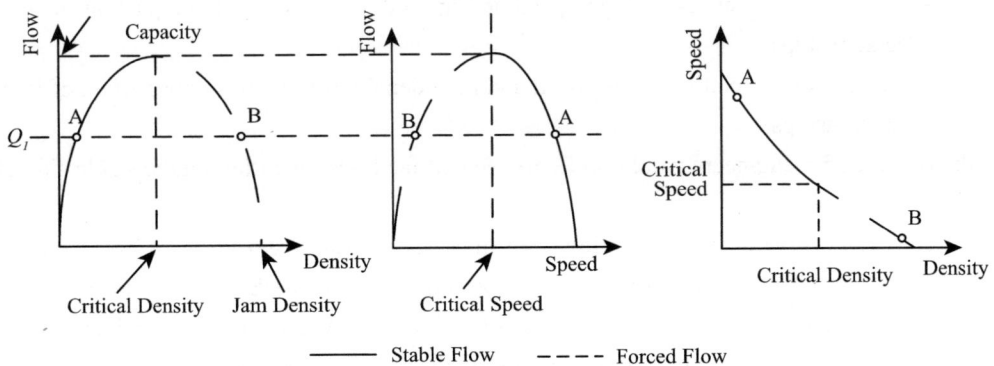

Figure 3.4   Relationships Among Flow, Speed and Density

Note that a flow rate of "0 veh/h" occurs under two very different conditions. When there are no vehicles on the highway, density is "0 veh/km" and no vehicles can be observed passing a point. Under this condition, speed is unmeasurable and is referred to as ***free-flow speed***" (V_f), a theoretical value that exists as a mathematical extension of the relationship between speed and flow (or speed and density). In practical terms, free-flow speed can be thought of as the speed a single vehicle can achieve when there are no other vehicles on the road and the motorist is driving as fast as is practicable given the geometry of the highway and its environmental surroundings.

A flow of "0 veh/h" also occurs when there are so many vehicles on the road that all motion stops. This occurs at a very high density, called the "***jam density***" (K_j), and no flow is observed, as no vehicle can pass a point to be counted when all vehicles are stopped.

Between these two extreme points in the relationships, there is a peaking characteristic. The peak of the flow-speed and flow-density curves is ***the maximum rate of flow, or the capacity of the roadway***. Its value, like everything else about these relationships, depends upon the specific prevailing conditions at the time and location of the calibration measurements. Operation at capacity, however, is very unstable. At capacity, with no usable gaps in the traffic stream, the slightest perturbation (扰动) caused by an entering or lane-changing vehicle, or simply a driver hitting the brakes, causes a chain reaction that cannot be damped. The perturbation propagates (传播) upstream and continues until sufficient gaps in the traffic stream allow the event to be effectively dissipated (消散).

The dashed portion of the curves represents unstable of forced flow. This effectively represents flow within a queue that has formed behind a breakdown location. A breakdown will occur at any point where the arriving flow rate exceeds the downstream capacity of the facility. Common points for such breakdowns include on-ramps on freeways, but accidents and incidents are also common, less predictable causes for the formation of queues. The solid line portion of the curves represents stable flow (i.e., moving traffic streams that can be maintained over a period of time).

Except for capacity flow, any flow rate may exist under two conditions:
- a condition of relatively high speed and low density (on the stable portion of flow relationships);
- a condition of relatively low speed and high density (on the unstable portion of flow relationships).

Obviously, traffic engineers would prefer to keep all facilities operating on the stable side of the curves.

Because a given volume or flow rate may occur under two very different sets of operating conditions, these variables con not completely describe flow conditions, nor can they be used as measures of the quality of traffic flow. Values of speed and/or density, however, would define unique points in any of the relationships of Figure 3.4, and both describe aspects of quality that can be perceived by drivers and passengers.

3.6.2 Greenshield's Linear Model

Over the years, various researchers have studied speed-flow-density relationships and have attempted to develop many mathematical descriptions for these curves. In the 1930s, Bruce Greenshields conducted the first formal studies of traffic stream. He hypothesized that the speed-density relationship was linear. Later, Greenberg hypothesized a logarithmic curve for speed-density, while Underwood used an exponential model for this relationship.

All of these historic studies focused on calibration of the speed-density relationship. This is considered to be the basic behavioral relationship—drivers selecting speeds based on their proximity to other vehicles (and the geometric and general environment of the roadway). Flow rate results from this relationship. Mathematically, once the speed-density relationship has been established, the speed-flow and flow-density relationships may be derived.

Consider Greenshield's linear speed-density model (Figure 3.5), selected for its simplicity. Mathematical models for speed-density may be manipulated to determine (a) free-flow speed, (b) jam density, and (c) capacity. Free-flow speed occurs when the density is "0 veh/h." Similarly, jam density occurs when the speed is "0 km/h".

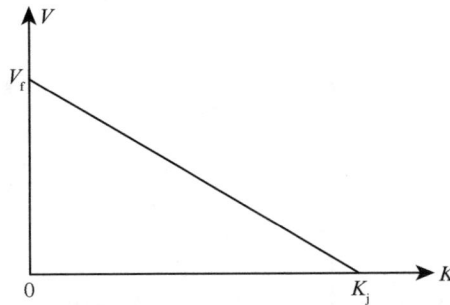

Figure 3.5　Greenshield's Linear Speed-density Model

Greenshield's linear speed-density model is computed by Equation 3.13:

$$V = V_f(1 - \frac{K}{K_j}) \tag{3.13}$$

where:

V — space mean speed, km/h;

K — density, veh/km or veh/km/ln;

V_f — the free-flow speed (畅行速度，自由流速度), km/h;

K_j — the jam density (阻塞密度), veh/km or veh/km/ln.

Knowing the general relationship, speed-flow and flow-density relationships can be derived by substitution:

$$Q = V \times K = -\frac{V_f}{K_j}K^2 + V_f K \Rightarrow Q(K) = -\frac{V_f}{K_j}K^2 + V_f K \tag{3.14}$$

Capacity is found by determining the peak of the speed-flow or flow-density curves. The peak occurs when the first derivative of the relationship is 0. Using the flow-density curve:

$$\frac{\mathrm{d}Q(K)}{\mathrm{d}K} = -2\frac{V_f}{K_j}K + V_f \qquad (3.15)$$

$$\frac{\mathrm{d}Q(K)}{\mathrm{d}K} = 0 \Rightarrow \begin{cases} K_m = \dfrac{K_j}{2} \\[2mm] V_m = \dfrac{V_f}{2} \\[2mm] Q_m = \dfrac{V_f K_j}{4} \end{cases} \qquad (3.16)$$

where

K_m — the ***critical density***, veh/km or veh/km/ln;

V_m — the ***critical speed***, km/h;

Q_m — the maximum rate of flow, or the capacity of the roadway.

This is the capacity of the section, based on the calibrated linear speed-density relationship for the section. Relationships of capacity-speed-density are illustrated as Figure 3.6.

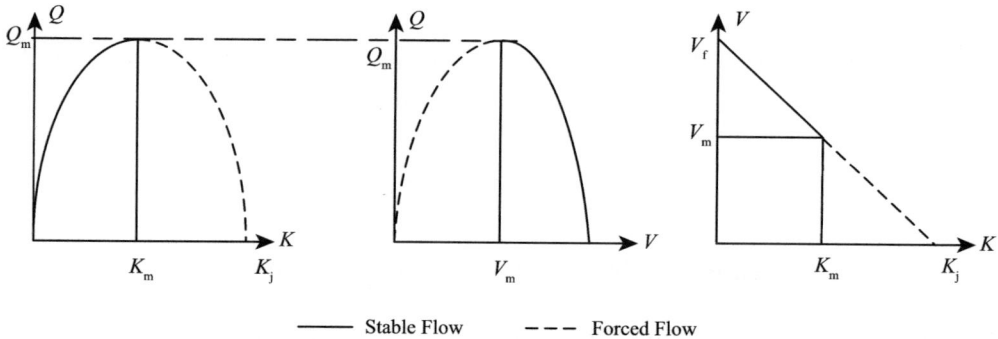

— Stable Flow　– – – Forced Flow

Figure 3.6　The Relationship Between Flow, Density, and Speed Based on Greenshield's Linear Model

It should be noted that there is no consensus as to which mathematical description best describes an uninterrupted-flow traffic stream. Indeed, studies suggest that the best form may vary by location and even over time at a given location. The linear model of Bruce Greenshields, originally calibrated in the 1930s, does not represent modern traffic behavior particularly well.

Exercises

1. Define the macroscopic parameters of a traffic stream: volume, speed, and density.
2. Define the microscopic parameters of a traffic stream: spacing and headway.
3. Monthly volume is listed below (Table 3.4). Try to calculate a) the max of ADT and AWT, and b) AADT and AAWT.

Table 3.4 Monthly Volume

Month	Number of Weekdays in Month (days)	Total Days in Month (days)	Total Monthly Volume (vehs)	Total Weekday Volume (vehs)
Jan.	22	31	302,548	215,642
Feb.	21	29	352,145	231,524
Mar.	22	31	365,289	234,589
Apr.	22	30	358,245	237,458
May	21	31	295,685	225,478
Jun.	22	30	368,549	225,486
Jul.	23	31	306,894	215,647
Aug.	21	31	354,896	224,869
Sep.	22	30	348,426	224,587
Oct.	22	31	347,125	224,756
Nov.	21	30	346,510	234,587
Dec.	22	31	361,202	231,046

4. Rate of flow is listed below (Table 3.5). Try to calculate PHF_5, PHF_{10} and PHF_{15}.

Table 3.5 Rates of Flow from 7:00 to 8:00

Interval	Volume	Interval	Volume
7:00 – 7:05	20	7:30 – 7:35	17
7:05 – 7:10	25	7:35 – 7:40	35
7:10 – 7:15	18	7:40 – 7:45	28
7:15 – 7:20	42	7:45 – 7:50	30
7:20 – 7:25	40	7:50 – 7:55	26
7:25 – 7:30	25	7:55 – 8:00	20

5. Observing the road section with a length of 100 m on the spot, the data is shown in Table 3.6. Try to calculate the average driving time, TMS and SMS.

Table 3.6   Data of Speed and Travel Time Observed

Vehicle No.	1	2	3	4	5	6	7	8
Travel time (s)	4.8	5.1	4.9	5.0	5.2	5.0	4.7	4.8
Speed (km/h)	75.0	70.6	73.5	72.0	69.2	72.0	76.6	75.0

6. On a circular road with a circumference of 1 km, there are 4 cars A, B, C and D, driving at a constant speed of 20 km/h, 40 km/h, 60 km/h and 80 km/h, respectively. Assuming free overtaking, ignoring distance and time changes during overtaking. Try to compute: a) Observe a fixed Point P on the loop for 1 h, find the flow rate at the section? b) TMS at Point P? c) SMS of all cars passing through Point P within 1 hour? 4) If each car has only been driven for a round, what is the ratio of the total travel of the 4 cars to the total time?

7. A traffic flow displays average vehicle headways of 2.2 s at 50 km/h. Compute the density and rate of flow for this traffic flow.

8. A freeway detector records an occupancy of 0.255 for a 15-minute period. If the detector is 0.9 m long, and the average vehicle has a length of 7.5 m, what is the density implied by this measurement?

9. On a 30 km long road section, 60 cars are measured within 5 minutes, and the traffic flow is uniform and continuous, V=30 km/h. What are the rate of flow, spacing, headway and density within an hour?

10. It is known that the free-flow velocity on a highway is 80 km/h, and the blocking density is 100 vehs/km. The relationship between speed and density conforms to the linear relationship of Greenshield. What is the maximum traffic volume expected on the road? What is the corresponding speed?

11. Assume that the speed-density model of traffic flow is V=88−1.6K. If the actual flow of traffic flow is limited to 0.8 time of the maximum flow, please calculate the lowest value of speed and the highest value of density ($K < K_m$).

Glossary

1. *Traffic streams (Traffic flow)*: 交通流, 指由单个驾驶员与车辆组成, 以独特的方式在车辆间、道路要素以及总体环境之间产生影响。

2. *Traffic volume*: 交通量，在选定时间段内，通过道路某一地点、某一断面或某一条车道的交通实体数。按交通类型分，有机动车交通量、非机动车交通量和行人交通量，一般不加说明则指机动车交通量，且指来往两个方向的车辆数。

3. *Rate of flow*: 流率，在不足1h时间间隔内，通过的车辆数除以观测时间（单位为h），所得即流率。

4. *Speed*: 车速，即距离与通过该距离所用时间之比。

5. *Density*: 密度，某一瞬间内单位道路长度上的车辆数。

6. *Headway*: 车头时距，前后两辆车通过车行道上某一点的时间差。

7. *Spacing*: 车头间距，同一车道上行驶的连续车辆中，前后两车车头之间的距离。

8. *STOP sign*: 停车让行标志，表示车辆必须在进入路口前完全停止，确认安全后，方可通行；停车让行标志宜单独设置。

9. *YIELD sign*: 减速让行标志，表示相交道路有优先通行权，车辆应慢行或停车，观察相交道路行车情况，让相交道路车辆优先通行并确认安全时，方可通行；减速让行标志宜单独设置。

10. *Uninterrupted flow facilities*: 连续流设施，指无外部因素会导致交通流周期性中断；主要指高速公路及一些限制出入口的路段。

11. *Interrupted flow facilities*: 间断流设施，指那些由于外部设备而导致交通流周期性中断的设施。

12. *AADT (Average Annual Daily Traffic)*: 年平均日交通量，一年内观测的交通量总和除以一年的总天数（365或366）。

13. *AAWT (Average Annual Weekday Traffic)*: 年平均工作日交通量，一年内观测的工作日交通量总和除以一年内工作日的总天数。

14. *ADT (Average Daily Traffic)*: 平均日交通量，将观测期间内统计的交通量总和除以观测总天数。

15. *AWT (Average Weekday Traffic)*: 平均工作日交通量，将观测期内统计的工作日交通量总和除以工作日总天数。

16. *The peak-hour volume*: 高峰小时交通量，一天内的高峰期间连续60min的最大交通量，单位为辆/h。

17. *Reversible lanes*: 潮汐车道，或可变车道，指一种根据交通流量需求可改变车辆行驶方向的车道。

18. *DDHV (Directional Design Hour Volume)*: 单向设计小时交通量。

19. *PHF (Peak-Hour Factor)*: 高峰小时系数，指高峰小时交通量与高峰小时内某一时段的交通量扩大为高峰小时的交通量之比。

20. *Time Mean Speed (TMS)*: 时间平均车速，在单位时间内测得通过道路某断面各车辆的点车速，这些点速度的算术平均值，即为该断面的时间平均车速。

21. *Space Mean Speed (SMS)*: 空间平均车速，在某一特定瞬间，行驶于道路某一特定长度内的全部车辆的车速分布的平均值，当观测长度为一定时，其数值为地点车速观测值的调和平均值。

22. *Occupancy*: 占有率，分为时间占有率和空间占有率。时间占有率是指观测时段内车辆占用检测器的百分比，代表车辆的时间密集度；空间占有率是观测区段内车身长度总和与路段长度之比，用来表示交通流状态。

23. *Free-flow speed*: 畅行速度，或自由流速度，车流密度趋于零，车辆可以畅行无阻时的平均速度。

24. *Jam density*: 阻塞密度，车流密集到所有车辆无法移动（v=0）时的密度。

25. *Critical density*: 临界密度，最佳密度，流量达到极大时的密度。

26. *Critical speed*: 临界速度，最佳速度，流量达到极大时的速度。

27. *The maximum rate of flow, or the capacity of the roadway*: 极大流量，极限流量，或通行能力，指道路上某一点、某一车道或某一断面处，单位时间内可能通过的最大交通实体（车辆或行人）数。

Key Points

1. Briefly introduce the composition of macroscopic parameters and microscopic parameters of traffic flow characteristics.
   简介交通流特征的宏观参数和微观参数构成。

2. Briefly describe the definition of traffic volume, different types of traffic volume and their functions.
   简述交通量的定义、不同类型的交通量及其作用。

3. Briefly describe the definition of speed, different types of speed and their applications.
   简述速度的定义、不同类型的速度及其应用。

4. Briefly describe the definitions of density and occupancy.
   简述密度和占有率的定义。

5. Briefly describe the definitions and applications of spacing and headway.
   简述车头间距和车头时距的定义及其应用。

6. Briefly describe the relations between macroscopic parameters of traffic flow characteristics.
   简述交通流特征的宏观参数之间的关系。

Chapter 4

Traffic Control Devices

Traffic control devices are media by which traffic engineers communicate with drivers. Virtually every traffic law, regulation, or operating instruction must be communicated through the use of devices that fail into three broad categories:

- *traffic markings*;
- *traffic signs*;
- *traffic signals*.

The effective communication between traffic engineers and drivers is a critical link if safe and efficient traffic operations are to prevail. Traffic engineers have no direct control over any individual driver or group of drivers. If a motorman violated a RED signal while conducting a subway train, an automated braking system would force the train to stop anyway. If a driver violates a RED signal, only the hazards of conflicting vehicular and/or pedestrian flows would impede the maneuver. Thus, it is imperative (极重要的) that traffic engineers design traffic control devices that communicate uncomplicated messages clearly, in a way that encourages proper observance.

4.1   Traffic Markings

Traffic markings are the most plentiful traffic devices in use. They serve a variety of purposes and functions and fall into three broad categories:

- *longitudinal markings*;
- *transverse markings*;
- *object markers and delineators*.

Longitudinal and transverse markings are applied to the roadway surface using a variety of materials, the most common of which are paint and thermoplastic (热塑性的). Reflectorization (反光) for better night vision is achieved by mixing tiny glass beads in the paint or by applying a thin layer of glass beads over the wet pavement marking as it is placed. The latter provides high initial reflectorization, but the top layer of glass beads is more quickly worn-out. When glass beads are mixed into the paint before applications, some level of reflectorization is preserved as the marking wears. Thermoplastic is a naturally reflective material, and nothing needs to be added to enhance drivers' ability to see them at night.

Object markers and delineators are small object-mounted reflectors, which are classified as *other markings* in China. Object markers are used to denote obstructions either in or adjacent to the traveled way. Delineators are reflective devices mounted on the side of a roadway to help denote its alignment. They are particularly useful during inclement weather, where pavement edge markings may not be visible.

4.1.1   Colors and Patterns

Five marking colors are in current use: yellow, white, red, blue, and black. In general, they are used as follows.

- Yellow markings separate traffic traveling in opposite directions.
- White markings separate traffic traveling in the same direction and are used for all transverse markings.
- Red markings delineate roadways that will not be entered or used by the viewer of the marking.
- Blue markings are used to delineate parking spaces reserved for persons with disabilities.
- Black markings are used in conjunction with other markings on light pavements. To emphasize the pattern of the line, gaps between yellow or white markings are filled in with black to provide contrast and easier visibility.

Pattern is used in the application of traffic markings. In general, double solid, solid, dashed and broken lines are used.

A solid line prohibits or discourages crossing. A double solid line indicates maximum or special restrictions. A broken line indicates that crossing is permissible. A dotted line uses shorter line segments than a broken line. It provides trajectory guidance and often is used as a continuation of another type of line in a conflict area. Normally, line markings are 10 to 15 cm wide. Wide lines, which provide greater emphasis, should be at least twice the width of a normal line. Broken lines normally consist of 4 m line segments and 6 m gaps. Similar dimensions with a similar ratio of line segments to gaps may be used as appropriate for prevailing traffic speeds and the need for delineation. Dotted lines usually consist of 2 m line segments and 4 m (or longer) gaps (Figure 4.1).

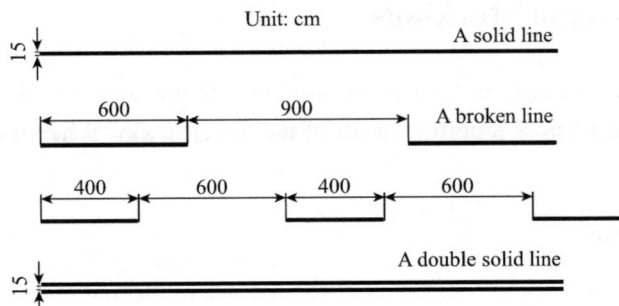

Figure 4.1   Illustrations of Broken Lines and Dotted Lines

4.1.2   Longitudinal Markings

Longitudinal markings are those markings placed parallel to the direction of travel. The vast majority of longitudinal markings involve centerlines, lane lines and pavement edge lines.

Longitudinal markings provide guidance for the placement of vehicles on the traveled way cross-section and basic trajectory guidance for vehicles traveling along the facility. The best example of the importance of longitudinal markings is the difficulty in traversing a newly paved highway segment on which lane markings have not yet been repainted. Drivers do not automatically form neat lanes without the guidance of longitudinal markings; rather, they tend to place themselves somewhat randomly on the cross-section, encountering many difficulties. Longitudinal markings provide for organized flow and optimal use of the pavement width.

(1) Centerlines

The yellow centerline marking is critically important and is used to separate traffic traveling in opposite directions. A double-solid yellow center marking indicates that passing is not permitted in either direction. A solid yellow line with a dashed yellow line indicates that passing is permitted from the dashed side only. Where passing is permissible in both directions, a single dashed yellow centerline is used.

(2) Lane Markings

The typical lane marking is a single white dashed line separating lanes of traffic in the same direction. The dashed lane line indicates that lane-changing is permitted. A single solid white lane line is used to indicate that lane-changing is prohibited.

(3) Edge Markings

Edge markings are used to indicate the edge of a motor lane or to demarcate the boundary between a motor lane and a non-motor lane.

4.1.3　Transverse Markings

Transverse markings, as their name implies, include any and all markings with a component that cuts across a portion or all of the traveled way. When used, all transverse markings are white.

(1) Stop Lines

In practice, stop lines are almost always used where marked crosswalks exist and in situations where the appropriate location to stop for a STOP sign or traffic signal is not clear. When used, stop lines must extend across all approach lanes.

(2) Crosswalk Markings

Crosswalks are recommended to be marked at all intersections at which "substantial" conflict between vehicles and pedestrians exists. They should also be used at points of pedestrian concentration and at locations where pedestrians might not otherwise recognize the proper place and/or path to cross.

(3) Parking Space Markings

Parking space markings are not purely transverse because they contain both longitudinal and transverse elements. They are officially categorized as transverse markings in the MUTCD ("US Manual on Uniform Traffic Control Devices",《美国统一交通控制设施设计手册》), while in China "Road Traffic Signs and Markings GB 5768.3—2022" specification, it is classified as other markings. They are always optional and are used to encourage efficient use of parking spaces. Such markings can also help prevent encroachment of parked vehicles into firehydrant zones, loading zones, taxi stands and bus stops, and other specific locations at which parking is prohibited. They are also useful on arterials with curb parking because they also clearly demark the parking lane, separating it from travel lanes (Figure 4.2).

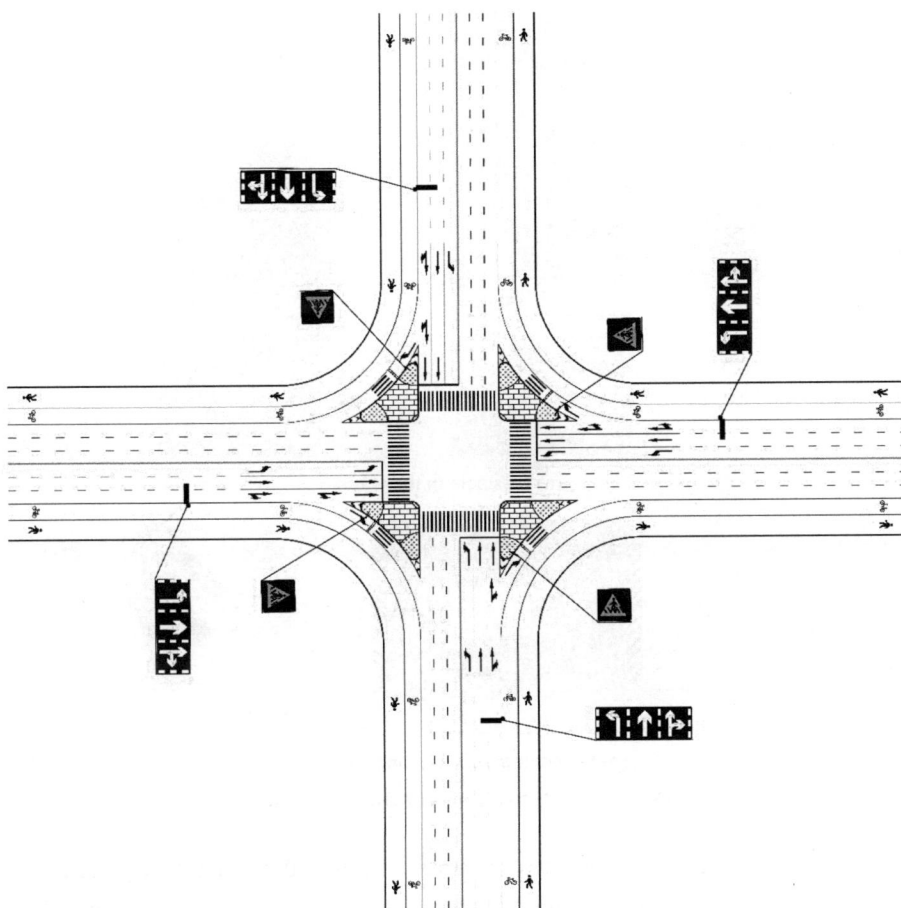

Figure 4.2   Illustrations of Longitudinal and Transverse Markings at an Intersection

(4) Word and Symbol Markings

A number of word and symbol markings are often used in conjunction with signs and/or signals. These include arrow markings indicating lane-use restrictions. Such arrows (with accompanying signs) are mandatory where a through lane becomes a left or right-turn-only lane approaching an intersection.

(5) Other Transverse Markings

Other types of transverse markings include preferential lane markings, curb markings, roundabout and traffic circle markings, and speed-hump markings.

4.1.4 Object Markers and Delineators

Object markers are used to denote obstructions either in or adjacent to the traveled way (Figure 4.3).

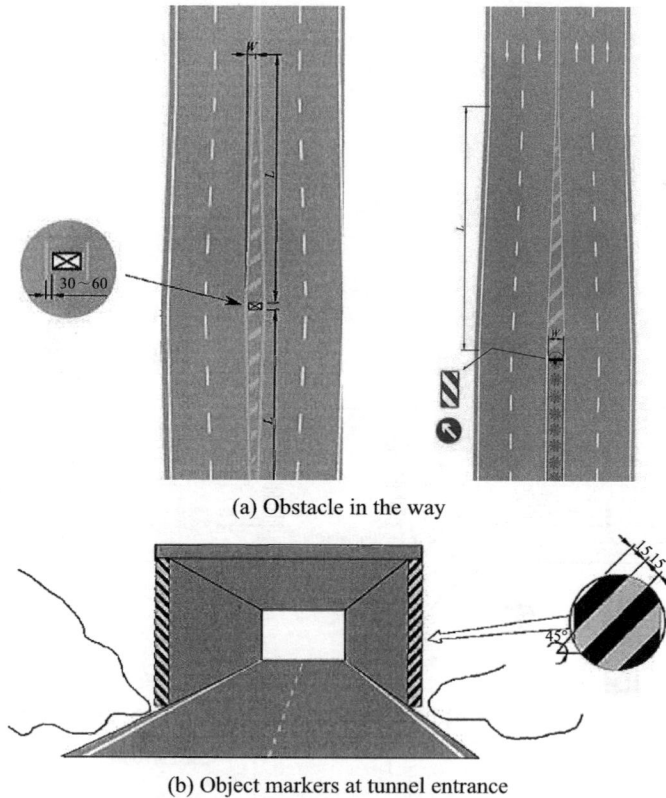

(a) Obstacle in the way

(b) Object markers at tunnel entrance

Figure 4.3   Illustrations of Object Markers

Delineators are reflective devices mounted at a 60-70 cm height on the side(s) of a roadway to help denote its alignment (Figure 4.4). They are particularly useful during inclement weather (恶劣天气) when pavement edge markings may not be visible.

Figure 4.4   Illustrations of Delineators

4.2   Traffic Signs

"Road Traffic Signs and Markings GB 5768.2—2022" of China provides specifications and guidelines for the use of literally hundreds of different signs for myriad purposes. In general, traffic signs fall into two major categories, primary traffic signs (主标志) and auxiliary traffic signs (辅助标志). Among them, primary traffic signs can be further subdivided into regulatory signs, warning signs, mandatory signs, guide signs, tourist area signs, and notice signs.

4.2.1   Regulatory Signs

Regulatory signs convey information concerning specific traffic regulations. Regulations may relate to right-of-way, speed limit, lane usage, parking, or a variety of other functions. Regulatory signs shall be used to inform road users of elected traffic laws or regulations and indicate the applicability of the legal requirements. Regulatory signs shall be installed at or near where the regulations apply (Figure 4.5).

(a) No Entry Sign   (b) Speed Limit Sign   (c) No Parking Sign

Figure 4.5   Illustrations of Regulatory Signs

(1) Regulatory Signs Affecting Right-of-Way

The regulatory signs in this category have special designs reflecting the extreme danger that exists when one is ignored. These signs include the STOP and YIELD signs, which assign right-of-way at intersections, and WRONG WAY and ONE WAY signs, indicating directional flow.

(2) Speed Limit Signs

One of the most important issues in providing for safety and efficiency of traffic movement is the setting of appropriate speed limits. To be effective, a speed limit must be communicated to the driver and should be sufficiently enforced to engender general observance.

(3) Turn and Movement Prohibition Signs

Where right, left, and/or U-turns, or even through movements, are prohibited, one or more of the movement prohibition signs are used. In this category, international symbol signs are preferred. The traditional red circle with a bar is placed over an arrow indicating the movement to be banned.

(4) Land-Use Signs

Lane-use control signs are used wherever a given movement or movements are restricted and/or prohibited from designated lanes. Such situations include left-turn-only and right-turn-only lanes, two-way left-turn lanes on arterials, and reversible lanes.

(5) Parking Control Signs

Curb parking control is one of the more critical aspects of urban network management. The economic viability of business areas often depends on an adequate and convenient supply of on-street and off-street parking. At the same time, curb parking often interferes with through traffic and occupies space on the traveled way that might otherwise be used to service moving traffic.

4.2.2   Warning Signs

Warning signs are used to inform drivers about upcoming hazards that they might not see or otherwise discern in time to react safely. Warning signs call attention to unexpected conditions on or adjacent to a highway or street, public facility, or private property open to public travel, and to situations that might not be readily apparent to road users. Warning signs alert road users to conditions that might call for a reduction of speed or an action in the interest of safety and efficient traffic operations (Figure 4.6).

The MUTCD indicates that warning signs shall be used only in conjunction with

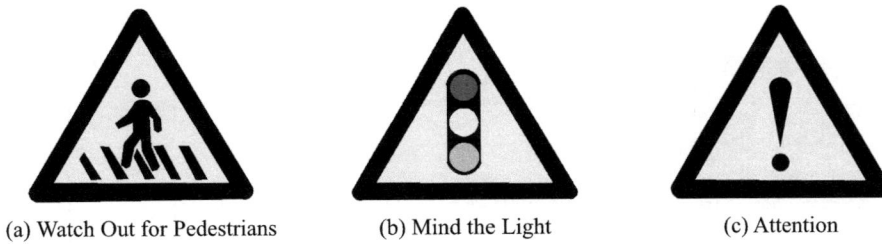

(a) Watch Out for Pedestrians　　(b) Mind the Light　　(c) Attention

Figure 4.6　Illustrations of Warning Signs

an engineering study or based on engineering judgment. Although this is a fairly loose requirement, it emphasizes the need to avoid overuse of such signs. A warning sign should be used only to alert drivers of conditions that they could not be normally expected to discern on their own. Overuse of warning signs encourages drivers to ignore them, which could lead to dangerous situations.

　　When used, warning signs must be placed far enough in advance of the hazard to allow drivers adequate time to perform the required adjustments.

4.2.3　Mandatory Signs and Guide Signs

　　Mandatory signs provide action instruction to vehicles and pedestrians that road users should follow (Figure 4.7). *Guide signs* provide information to road users on routes, destinations, and services that drivers may be concerned (Figure 4.8). Mandatory signs and guide signs have some similarities in function, but they are also different in essence.

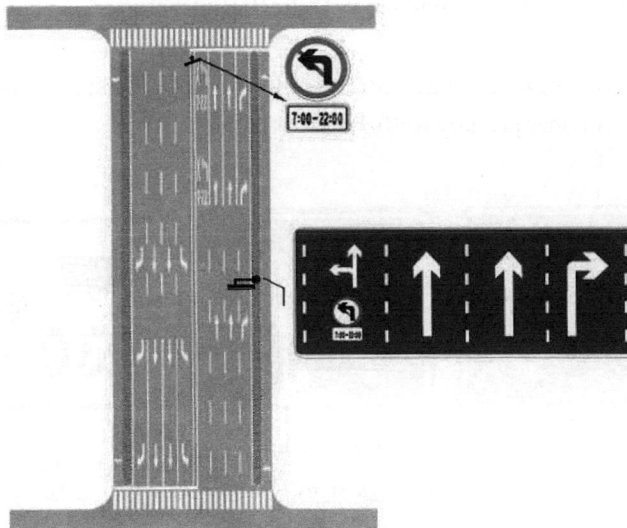

Figure 4.7　Illustrations of Mandatory Signs

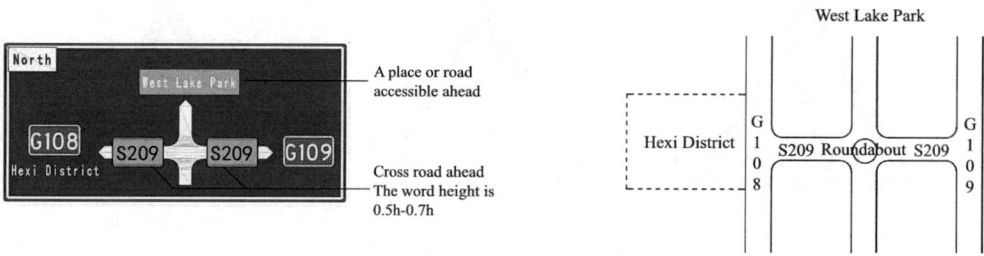

Figure 4.8　Illustrations of Guide Signs

Similarities: They all serve traffic information to road users. Most of signs have white lettering and a blue background.

Differences: Mandatory signs contains basic travel rules, which are always used in conjunction with regulatory signs that road users have to follow. On the other hand, guide signs serve a unique purpose in that drivers who are familiar or regular users of a route will generally not need to use them; they provide critical information, however, to unfamiliar road users.

4.2.4　Other Traffic Signs

Tourist area signs are designed to attract and guide people from highways or other roads to neighboring tourist areas. Signs are set up at the intersection leading to tourist attractions, which may include information of the direction and distance to the tourist area and the types of tourist projects (Figure 4.9).

Notice signs are used to announce road traffic interruption, travel information and other information.

Auxiliary traffic signs provide more detail information about primary traffic signs, which have to be set under primary traffic signs (Figure 4.10).

(a) Yunjusi　　　　　(b) Hiking

Figure 4.9　Illustrations of Tourist Area Signs

Figure 4.10　Illustrations of Auxiliary Traffic Signs

4.3 Traffic Signals

The MUTCD defines nine types of traffic signal:

- traffic control signals;
- pedestrian signals;
- emergency vehicle traffic control signals;
- traffic control signals for one-lane, two-way facilities;
- traffic control signals for freeway entrance ramps;
- traffic control signals for moveable bridges;
- lane-use control signals;
- flashing beacons;
- in-roadway lights.

The most common of these is the traffic control signal, used at busy intersections to direct traffic to alternately stop and move.

4.3.1 Traffic Control Signals

Traffic signals are the most complicated form of traffic control devices available to traffic engineers. The MUTCD specifies two critical standards with respect to traffic control signals (Figure 4.11)

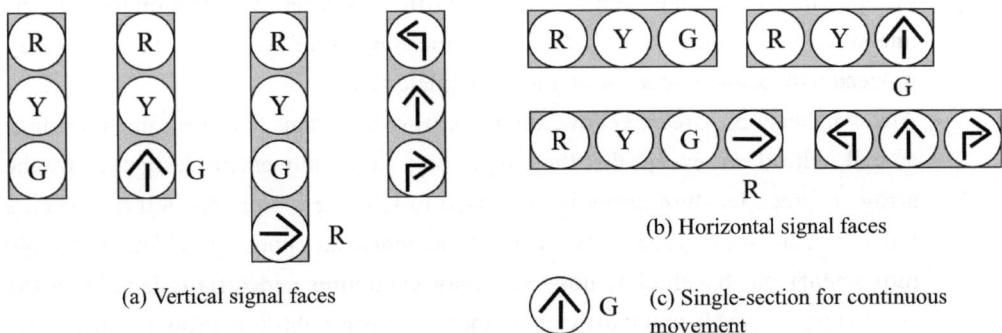

Figure 4.11 Illustrations of Traffic Control Signals

A traffic control signal shall be operated in either a steady-state (stop and go) mode or a flashing mode at all times. No traffic signal should ever be "dark", that is, showing no indications. This is particularly confusing to drivers and can result in accidents. Any accidents occurring while a signal is in the dark mode are the legal responsibility of the agency operating the signal in most states. When signals are inoperable, signal heads should be bagged or taken down to avoid such confusion. In power outages, police or other authorized agents should be used to direct traffic at all signalized locations.

STOP signs shall not be used in conjunction with any traffic control signal operation except in either of the two following cases: (a) if the signal indication for an approach is a flashing red at all times; and (b) if a minor street or driveway is located within or adjacent to the area controlled by the traffic control signal, but does not require separate traffic signal control because an extremely low potential for conflict exist.

The MUTCD defines the meaning of each traffic control signal indication as follows.

- Green ball. A steady green circular indication allows vehicular traffic facing the ball to enter the intersection to travel straight through the intersection or to turn right or left, except when prohibited by lane-use controls or physical design. Turning vehicles must yield the right-of-way to opposing through vehicles and to pedestrians legally in a conflicting crosswalk. In the absence of pedestrian signals, pedestrians may proceed to cross the roadway within any legally marked or unmarked crosswalk.
- Yellow ball. The steady yellow circular indication is a transition between the Green Ball and the Red Ball indication. It warns drivers that the related green movement is being terminated or that a red indication will immediately follow. Where no pedestrian signals in use, pedestrians may not begin crossing a street during the "yellow" indication.
- Red ball. The steady red circular indication requires all traffic (vehicular and pedestrian) facing it to stop at the STOP line, crosswalk line (if no STOP line exists), or at the conflicting pedestrian path (if no crosswalk or STOP line exists). Right-turning traffic is allowed to proceed with caution after stopping, unless specifically prohibited by signing or statute.
- Flashing ball. A flashing "yellow" allows traffic to proceed with caution through the intersection. A flashing "red" has the same meaning as a STOP sign—the driver may proceed with caution after coming to a complete stop.
- Arrow indications. Green, yellow, and red arrow indications have the same meanings as ball indications, except that they apply only to the movement designated by the arrow. A green left-turn arrow is only used to indicate a protected left turn (i.e., a left turn made on a green arrow will not encounter an opposing vehicular through movement). Such vehicles, however, may encounter pedestrians legally in the conflicting crosswalk and must yield to them. A green right-turn arrow is shown only when there are no pedestrians legally in the conflicting crosswalk. Yellow arrows warn drivers that the green arrow is about to terminate.

4.3.2   Pedestrian Signals

The millennium edition of the MUTCD has mandated the use of new pedestrian signals that have been introduced as options over the past several years. The use of the older "WALK" and "DON'T WALK" designs has been discontinued in favor of the following indication.

- Walking man (steady). The new "WALK" indication is the image of a walking person in the color of white. This indicates that it is permissible for a pedestrian to enter the crosswalk to begin crossing the street.
- Upraised hand (flashing). The new "DON'T WALK" indication is an upraised hand in the color Portland orange. In the flashing mode, it indicates that no pedestrian may enter the cross-walk to begin crossing the street but that those already crossing may continue safely.
- Upraised hand (steady). In the steady mode, the upraised hand indicates that no pedestrian should begin crossing and that no pedestrian should still be in the crosswalk.

In previous manuals, a flashing "WALK" indication was an option that could be used to indicate that a right-turning vehicle may be conflicting with pedestrians legally in the crosswalk. The new manual does not permit a flashing WALKING MAN, effectively discontinuing this practice (Figure 4.12).

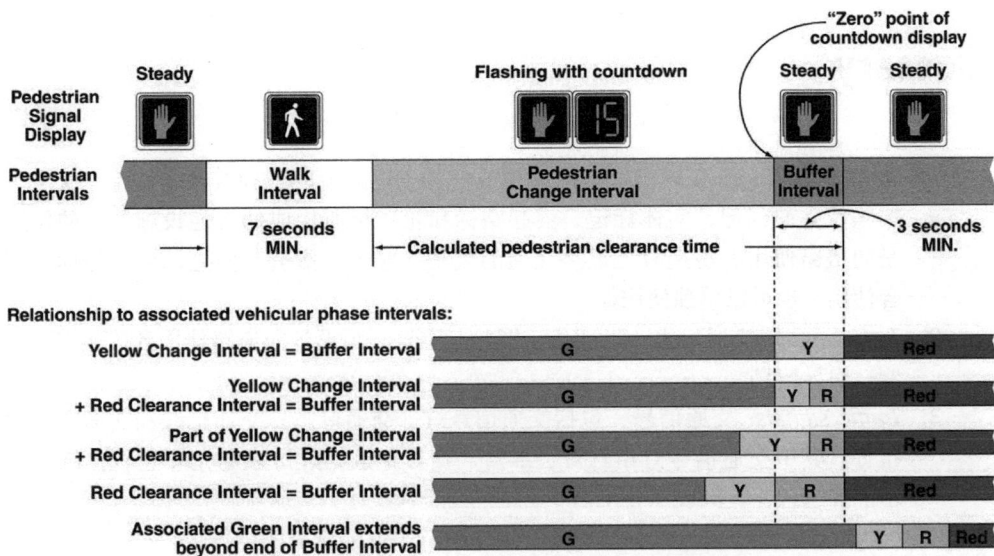

Figure 4.12   Illustrations of Pedestrian Signals

4.3.3   Other Traffic Signals

The MUTCD provides specific criteria for the design, placement, and use of a number of other types of signals, including:

- beacons;
- in-roadway lights;
- lane-use control signals;
- ramp control signals (or ramp meters).

Beacons are generally used to identify a hazard or call attention to a critical control device, such as a speed limit sign, a STOP or YIELD sign, or a DO NOT ENTER sign. Lane-use control signals are used to control reversible lanes on bridge, in tunnels, and on streets and highways.

Exercises

1. What are the objectives of traffic control devices?
2. Define the following terms: traffic marking, traffic signs, traffic signals.
3. Describe the categories of traffic marking, traffic signs, and traffic signals.
4. What is the difference between mandatory signs and guide signs?

Glossary

1. *Traffic markings*: 交通标线，由施划或安装于道路上的各种线条、箭头、文字、图案及立面标记、实体标记、突起路标和轮廓标所构成的交通设施，它的作用是向道路使用者传递有关道路交通的规则、警告、指引等信息，可以与标志配合使用，也可以单独使用。
2. *Traffic signs*: 交通标志，以颜色、形状、字符、图形等向道路使用者传递交通控制、引导信息。
3. *Traffic signals*: 交通信号，包括交通信号灯、交通标志、交通标线和交通警察的指挥。其中交通信号灯由红灯、绿灯、黄灯组成；红灯表示禁止通行，绿灯表示准许通行，黄灯表示警示。
4. *Longitudinal markings*: 纵向标线，沿道路行车方向设置的标线。
5. *Transverse markings*: 横向标线，与道路行车方向交叉设置的标线。
6. *Object markers*: 物标，实体标记，用以给出道路净空范围内实体构造物的轮廓，提醒驾驶人注意。
7. *Delineators*: 反光标，或突起路标，是固定于路面上起标线作用的突起标记块，可用来标记对向车行道分界线、同向车行道分界线、车行道边缘线等，也可用来标记弯道、进出口匝道、导流标线、道路变窄、路面障碍物等危险路段。
8. *Other markings*: 其他标线，字符标记或其他形式标线。
9. *Regulatory signs*: 禁令标志，禁止或限制道路使用者交通行为的标志。
10. *Warning signs*: 警告标志，警告道路使用者注意道路、交通的标志。
11. *Mandatory signs*: 指示标志，指示道路使用者应遵循的标志。
12. *Guide signs*: 指路标志，传递道路方向、地点、距离信息的标志。

13. *Tourist area signs*：旅游区标志，提供旅游景点方向、距离的标志。

14. *Notice signs*：告示标志，告知路外设施、安全行驶信息以及其他信息的标志。

15. *Auxiliary traffic signs*：辅助交通标志，设在主标志下方，对其进行辅助说明的标志。

Key Points

1. Briefly describe the functions and types of traffic control devices.
   简述交通控制设施的功能和类型。

2. Briefly describe the types and functions of traffic markings.
   简述交通标线的类型和作用。

3. Briefly describe the types and functions of traffic signs.
   简述交通标志的类型和作用。

4. Briefly describe the types and functions of traffic signals.
   简述交通信号的类型和作用。

Chapter 5

Traffic Management

5.1 Intersection Control

There are many types of intersections, which are mainly divided into two categories: *at-grade intersections* and *grade separations* (Figure 5.1).

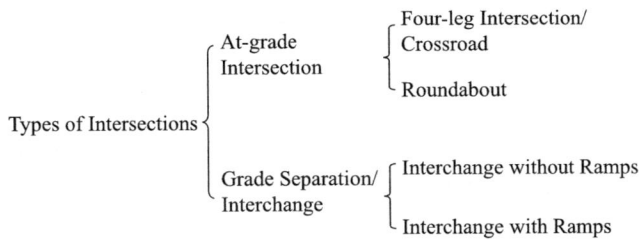

Figure 5.1 Types of Intersections

The most complex individual locations within any street and highway system are at-grade intersections. At a typical intersection of a two-way street, there are 12 legal vehicular movements (left turn, through, and right turn from four approaches) and four legal pedestrian crossing movements. As indicated in Figure 5.2, these movements create many potential conflicts where vehicles and/or pedestrian paths may try to occupy the same physical space at the same time.

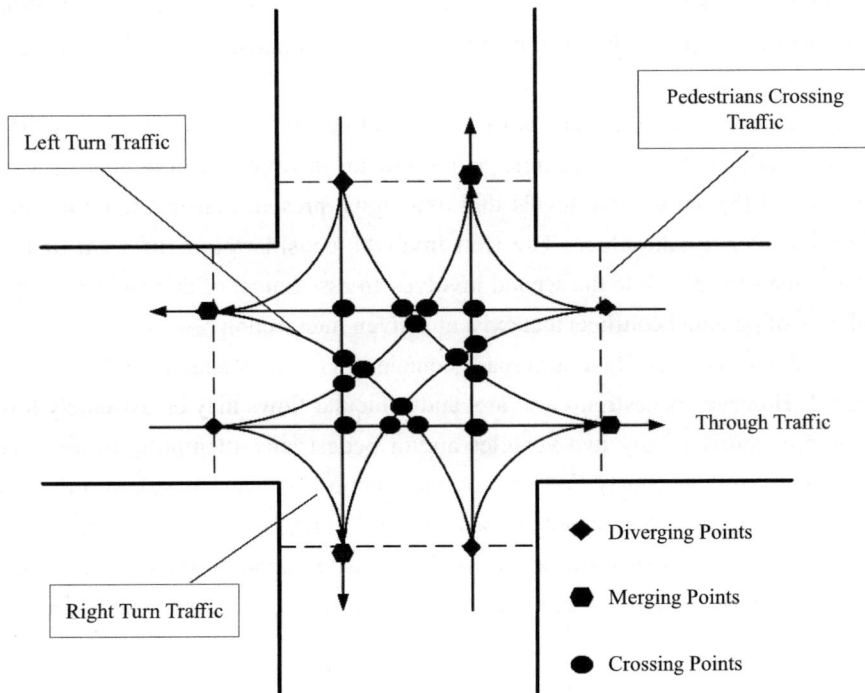

Figure 5.2 Conflicts at a Typical At-Grade Intersection

Vehicular movements conflicts are divided into three categories: diverging, merging, and crossing points. As illustrated in Figure 5.2, there are eight vehicular *diverging conflicts*, as vehicles diverge into left-turning, through or right-turning vehicles. There are a total of 16 potential vehicular *crossing conflicts*: four between through movements from the two streets, four between left-turning movements from the two streets, and eight between left-turning movements and through movements from the two streets. In addition, there are eight vehicular *merging conflicts*, as right-and left-turning vehicles merge into a through flow at the completion of their desired maneuver. Pedestrians add additional potential conflicts to the mix.

The critical task of the traffic engineer is to control and manage these conflicts in a manner that ensures safety and provides for efficient movement through the intersection for both motorists and pedestrians.

5.1.1　Hierarchy of Intersection Control

There are three basic levels of control that can be implemented at an intersection:
- Level Ⅰ—Basic rules of the road;
- Level Ⅱ—Direct assignment of right-of-way using YIELD or STOP signs;
- Level Ⅲ—Traffic signalization.

There are variations within each level of control as well. The selection of an appropriate level of control involves a determination of which (and how many) conflicts a driver should be able to perceive and avoid through the exercise of judgment. Where it is not reasonable to expect a driver to perceive and avoid a particular conflict, traffic controls must be imposed to assist.

Two factors affect a driver's ability to avoid conflicts: (a) a driver must be able to see a potentially conflicting vehicle or pedestrian in time to implement an avoidance maneuver and (b) the volume levels that exist must present reasonable opportunities for a safe maneuver to take place. The first involves considerations of sight distance and avoidance maneuvers, while the second involves an assessment of demand intensity and the complexity of potential conflicts that exist at a given intersection.

A rural intersection of two farm roads contains all of the potential conflicts illustrated in Figure 5.1. However, pedestrians are rare, and vehicular flows may be extremely low. There is a low probability of any two vehicles and/or pedestrians attempting to use a common physical point simultaneously (同时地). At the junction between two major urban arterials, the probability of vehicles or pedestrians on conflicting paths arriving simultaneously is quite high. The sections that follow discuss how a determination of an appropriate form of intersection control can be made, highlighting the important factors to consider in making such critical decisions.

5.1.2   Level Ⅰ Control: Basic Rules of the Road

Basic rules of the road apply at any intersection where ***right-of-way*** is not explicitly assigned through the use of traffic signals, STOP or YIELD signs. At intersections, drivers follow a similar format. Firstly, through vehicles have the right of way over turning vehicles at uncontrolled intersections. Secondly, in the absence of control devices, the driver on the left must yield to the driver on the right when the vehicle on the right is approaching in a manner that may create an impending hazard. In essence, the responsibility for avoiding a potential conflict is assigned to the vehicle on the left.

Operating under basic rules of the road does not imply that no control devices are in place at or in advance of the intersection, although that could be the case. Use of street-name signs, other guide signs, or advance intersection warning signs do not change the application of the basic rules. They may, however, be able to contribute to the safety of the operation by calling the driver's attention to the existence and location of the intersection.

In order to safely operate under basic rules of the road, drivers on conflicting approaches must be able to see each other in time to assess whether an "impending hazard" is imposed, and to take appropriate action to avoid an accident. Sight distances must be analyzed to ensure that they are sufficient for drivers to judge and avoid conflicts.

Even if the intersection meets the sight distance criteria, this does not mean that basic rules of the road should be applied to the intersection. Adequate sight distance is a necessary, but not sufficient, condition for adopting a "no-control" option. Traffic volumes or other conditions may make a higher level of control desirable or necessary.

In this intersection, sight distance must be analyzed to ensure that drivers can judge and avoid conflicts. The ***sight triangle*** at an intersection is illustrated in Figure 5.3.

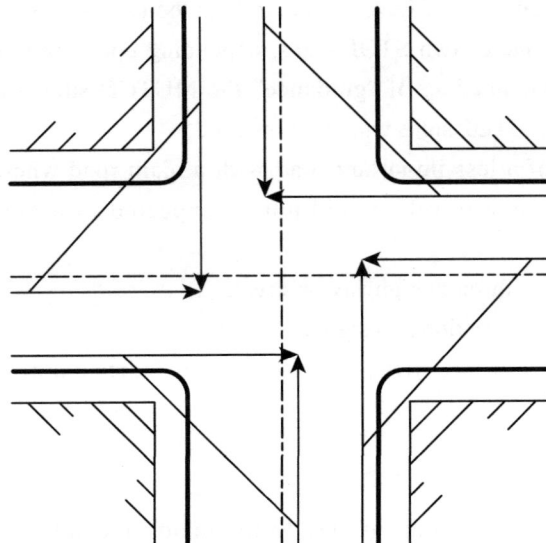

Figure 5.3   Sight Triangle at an Intersection

5.1.3   Level Ⅱ Control: YIELD and STOP Control

If a check of the intersection sight triangle indicates that it would not be safe to apply the basic rules of the road, then as a minimum, some form of Level Ⅱ control must be imposed. Even if sight distance is safe for operating under no control, there may be other reasons to implement a higher level of control as well. Usually, these would involve the intensity of traffic demand and the general complexity of the intersection environment (Figure 5.4).

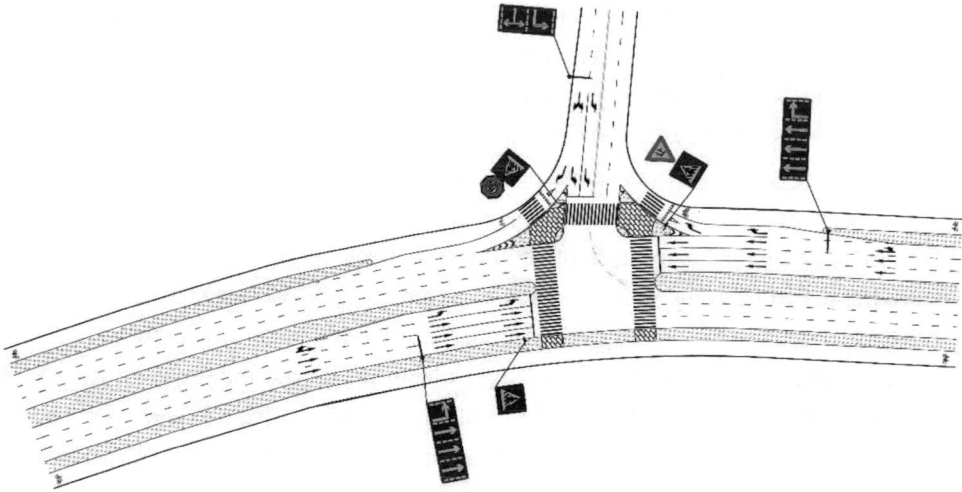

Figure 5.4   YIELD and STOP Control at an Intersection

(1) *Two-Way STOP Control*

The most common form of Level Ⅱ controls is the two-way STOP sign. In fact, such control may involve one or two STOP signs, depending upon the number of intersection approaches. Under the heading of "guidance" the MUTCD suggests several conditions under which the use of STOP signs would be justified.

- Intersection of a less important road with a main road where application of the normal right-of-way rule would not be expected to provide reasonably safe operation.
- Street entering a through highway or street.
- Unsignalized intersection in a signalized area.
- High speeds, restricted view, or crash records indicate a need for control by the STOP sign.

(2) YIELD Control

A YIELD sign assigns right-of-way to the major uncontrolled street. It requires vehicles on the minor approach to slow and yield the right-of-way to any major street vehicle approaching at a distance and speed that would present an impending hazard to minor street vehicle if it entered the major street. Most state laws require that drivers on YIELD-controlled approaches slow to 10-15 km/h before entering a major street.

Warrants for YIELD control are summarized as follows.

- When the ability to see all potentially conflicting traffic is sufficient to allow a road use traveling at the posted speed, 85th percentile speed, or the statutory speed to pass through the intersection or stop in a safe manner.
- If controlling a merge-type movement on the entering roadway where acceleration geometry or sight distance is not adequate for merging traffic operations.
- At a second crossroad of a divided highway, where the median width is 10m or greater. A STOP sign may be installed at the entrance to the first roadway of a divided highway, and a YIELD sign may be installed at the entrance to the second roadway.
- At an intersection where a special problem exists and where engineering judgment indicates that the problem is susceptible (易受……影响) to correction by use of a YIELD sign.

(3) Multi-Way STOP Control

Multi-way STOP control, where all intersection approaches are controlled using STOP signs, remains a controversial form of control. Some agencies find it attractive, primarily as a safety measure. Others believe that the confusion that drivers often exhibit under this form of control negates any of the benefits it might provide.

Multi-way STOP control is most often used where there are significant conflicts between vehicles, and pedestrians and/or bicyclists in all directions. And where vehicular demands on the intersecting roadways are approximately equal.

5.1.4   Level Ⅲ Control: Traffic Control Signal

The ultimate form of intersection control is the traffic signal. Because it alternately assigns right-of-way to specific movements, it can substantially reduce the number and nature of intersection conflicts as no other form of control can. Figure 5.5 illustrates a typical four-leg-intersection with traffic signals.

If drivers obey the signal, then driver judgment is not needed to avoid some of the most critical intersection conflicts. Imposition of traffic signal control does not, however, remove all conflicts from the realm of the driver's judgment.

(1) Advantages of Traffic Signal Control

The MUTCD lists the following advantages of traffic control signals that are "properly designed, located, and maintained." These advantages are as follows.

- They provide for the orderly movement of traffic.

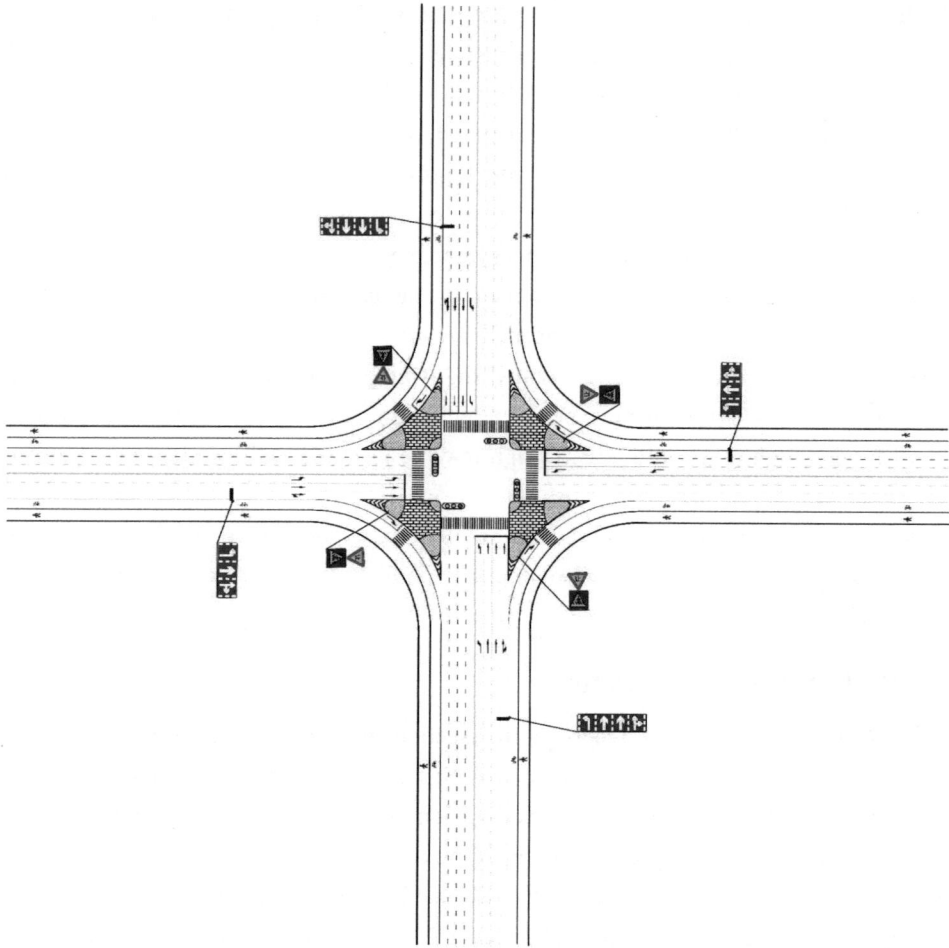

Figure 5.5   Traffic Signal Controlled Intersection

- They increase the traffic-handling capacity of the intersection if proper physical layouts and control measures are used and if the signal timing is reviewed and updated on a regular basis to ensure that it satisfies the current traffic demands.
- They reduce the frequency and severity of certain types of crashes, especially right-angle collision.
- They are coordinated to provide for continuous or nearly continuous movement at a definite speed along a given route under favorable conditions.
- They are used to interrupt heavy traffic at intervals to permit other traffic, vehicles or pedestrians, to cross.

These specific advantages address the primary reasons why a traffic signal would be installed: to increase capacity (thereby improving the *level of service*), to improve safety, and to provide for orderly movement through a complex situation. Coordination of signals provides other benefits, but not all signals are necessarily coordinated.

(2) Disadvantages of Traffic Signal Control

The description of the second advantage in the foregoing list indicates that capacity is increased by a well-designed signal at a well-designed intersection. Poor design of either the signalization or the intersection can significantly reduce the benefits achieved or negate them entirely. Improperly designed traffic signals, or the placement of a signal where it is not justified, can lead to some of the following disadvantages:

- excessive delay;
- excessive disobedience of the signal indications;
- increase use of less adequate routes as road users attempt to avoid the traffic control signal;
- significant increases in the frequency of collisions (especially rear-end collisions).

Item 4 is of some interest. Even when they are properly installed and well-designed, traffic signal controls can lead to increases in rear-end accidents because of the cyclical stopping of the traffic stream. Where safety is concerned, signals can reduce the number of right-angle, turning, and pedestrian/bicycle accidents; they might cause an increase in rear-end collisions (which tend to be less severe); they will have almost no impact on head-on or sideswipe accidents, or on single-vehicle accidents involving fixed objected.

Excessive delay can result from an improperly installed signal, but it can also occur if the signal timing is inappropriate. In general, excessive delay results from cycle lengths that are either too long or too short for the existing demands at the intersection. Further, drivers will tend to assure that a signal is broken if they experience an excessive wait, particularly when there is little or no demand occurring on the cross street.

5.2 Traffic System Management

According to the US Federal Road Authority Planning Ordinance, Traffic System Management (TSM) is treating the car, public transport, taxis, pedestrians and bicycles as an overall urban transport system of multiple components. The purpose of urban traffic system management is to coordinate these individual components to make this system as a whole in order to achieve maximum transport efficiency through the operation, management and service policies.

Traffic system management is a process for planning and operating a unitary system of urban transportation. Its key objective is conservation of fiscal resources of energy, environmental quality, and enhancement of the quality life. The federal regulations state that automobiles, public transportation, taxis, pedestrians, and bicycles should all be considered as elements of a single transportation system. The objective of TSM is to coordinate these individual elements through operating, regulating, and service policies so as to achieve maximum efficiency and productivity for the system as a whole.

5.2.1   Objectives and Characteristics

The main objectives of TSM are to maximize urban mobility within a given existing system through the development of specific applicable actions in the following four categories:

- actions to ensure efficient use of existing road space;
- actions to reduce vehicle use in congested areas;
- actions to improve transit service;
- actions to improve internal transit management efficiency.

Note that TSM actions should be consistent with efforts to conserve energy, improve air quality, and increase social, and environmental amenity. TSM actions cover all categories of improvements appropriate to a region, and the level of analysis should be scaled to the size of the urbanized area and to the magnitude of the transportation problems. Assessment of candidate measures (i.e., evaluation criteria) or selection, programming, and implementation fall under the purview of local prerogatives.

The characteristic of TSM: traditional traffic management focuses on the harmful effects of local traffic management measures in a single isolated, which can play a role in the mitigation of local traffic scourge, but it often diverts the harmful effects of the local traffic scourge to nearby areas. Furthermore, a single isolated traffic management measure may not be the optimal efficiency measure. The optimization of traffic system can only be realized by comprehensive system management, which can also reduce the negative effects of any single management measure.

5.2.2   Categories of the Basic Measures

In the United States and Western Europe, the widely used basic measures for the management of transport systems can be summarized into the following ten categories.

- Public transport auxiliary system. There are ridesharing vehicles, small buses, special buses, etc.
- Public transport operation and management. Improvement in traffic routes and schedules, improving the terminal and docking stations, opening up direct express train, improving the collection method, improving vehicle maintenance, improving the operation and monitoring, etc.
- The parking lot management. There is a roadside parting lot management and street cars external parking management, and transfer system, parking lot management, and priority to parking lot management, parking lot line guide.
- Pedestrians, bicycle management. There are pedestrians crossing streets, pedestrian

precinct areas, bike lanes, intersection of cycling management.

- Traffic restrictions. There are restrictions on vehicle areas, certificate into the area, pedestrian and bus traffic lane, traffic restrictions on residential areas and management.
- Access priority management. Improving the traffic monitoring of the intersection, one-way traffic, variable direction of lanes, traffic signal control system, etc.
- Traffic restraint measures. Restricting vehicle area, certificating area, pedestrian and bus traffic lane, traffic restrictions on residential areas, etc.
- Freight Traffic Management. Improving the routing, improving the loading and unloading operations, the establishment of cargo hubs, etc.
- Changing the method of working. Staggered working hours, implementation of flexible working system, working at home, etc.
- Charge management. Surcharging license fees, gasoline taxes, crossing the road toll, electronic toll collection, congestion pricing, pollution charges.

These are ten categories of measure, some are similar or mutually exclusive, only one is chosen, while some can complement each other, and combine in order to improve efficiency.

The technology of transportation system management is that around the existing conditions and crux of the problem of road transport system, choosing the relevant measures, combining them into a variety of comprehensive programs, and advancing optimal program according to the traffic benefit evaluation results.

The basic focus of transportation system management is to fully tap the role of the existing transport infrastructure and achieve maximum transport efficiency with minimal cost.

Exercises

1. Describe the conflicts of an intersection.
2. Describe the hierarchy of intersection control.
3. Illustrate the main measurements of traffic operation management.

Glossary

1. *At-grade intersections*: 平面交叉口，两条或两条以上的道路在同一平面相交称为平面交叉口。
2. *Grade intersections*: 立体交叉口，是指上下层道路之间互不相通的立体交叉形式。

3. *Diverging conflicts*: 分离冲突点，原本同一方向行驶的车流由于行驶方向不同而产生的分流点。

4. *Crossing conflicts*: 交叉冲突点，不同方向的车流由于相互穿行而存在的潜在交叉碰撞点。

5. *Merging conflicts*: 合流冲突点，不同行驶方向的车流汇聚到同一方向行驶而产生的合流点。

6. *Right-of-way*: 路权，交通参与者的权利，是交通参与者根据交通法规的规定，在一定空间和时间内在道路上进行道路交通活动的权利。

7. *Sight triangle*: 视距三角，常被用来分析交叉口上视距是否足够的一种图解分析方法。

8. *Two-way STOP control*: 两向停车方式，用于主要道路与次要道路相交路口。主要道路上的车辆优先通行，通过路口不用停车；次要道路上的车辆必须首先让主要道路上的车辆通行，寻找机会，穿越主要道路上车流的空档，通过路口。

9. *Multi-way STOP control*: 全向停车方式，相交道路具有同等重要程度，车辆通过交叉口具有同等的优先权，都必须在交叉口处停车，然后根据交通法规的规定，选择恰当时机通过。

10. *Level of service*: 服务水平，衡量交通流运行条件以及驾驶员和乘客所感受的服务质量的一项指标。

Key Points

1. Briefly describe the definition and types of intersection conflict.
简述交叉口冲突的定义和类型。

2. Briefly describe the intersection control types and control rules.
简述交叉口控制类型和控制规则。

3. Briefly describe the objectives and functions of traffic system management.
简述交通系统管理的目标和作用。

4. Briefly describe the types of traffic system management.
简述交通系统管理的类型。

Chapter 6

Transportation Planning

The urban transportation system is a basic component of an urban area's social, economic, and physical structure. ***Transportation planning*** is considered to be an important function in modern society and it is concentrated in particular areas, subjects, or systems. Not only does the design and performance of a transportation system provide opportunities for mobility, but over the long term, it influences patterns of growth and the level of economic activity through the accessibility it provides to land.

The conception of transportation planning has been given by many researchers. In generally, transportation planning can be seen as an act of laying out a transportation system aiming to predict the needs and demands for a particular service. Or it can be defined as the process of making decisions related to the future of the transportation system. Or it can be defined as a process whose objective, in a broad sense, is to develop a system of transport which will enable people and goods to travel safely and economically. Transportation planning recognizes the critical links between transportation and other societal goals, and plays a fundamental role in the state, region or community vision for its future.

Transportation planning can be a highly technical process, which often relies on computer models and other underlined sophisticated (精密的) tools to simulate the complex interactions of transportation system performance. It is a public relationship-oriented process in that transportation planners often interact with a wide range of stakeholders and members of the public. Transportation planning can also become intertwined (错综复杂的) with the politics of any given decision.

Some transportation planners and engineers focus on transportation supply—the facilities and services needed to handle expected demands and characteristics of the infrastructure to provide such service. Others are more interested in influencing travel behavior to promote more cost-effective and environmentally sustainable options for travelers.

6.1　Fundamentals of Transportation Planning

6.1.1　Goals of Transportation Planning

Transportation planning focuses on issues such as the future demand for transportation; interaction among different transportation systems and facilities; the relationships among land use, economic activity, and transportation; alternative ways of operating transportation systems; the social, economic, and environmental impacts of proposed transportation systems; and the financial and institutional arrangements needed to implement transportation proposals. Discussions of transportation planning may focus on either the various methodologies involved or on the institutional aspects of the planning process.

Transportation planning should strive to the following criteria listed below:

- serving for more people or goods;

- faster;
- safe;
- cheap;
- minimizing pollution;
- promoting better land development.

A planning activity occurs during one time period but is concert with actions to be taken at various times in the future. However, although planning may increase the likelihood that a recommended action will in fact take place, it does not guarantee that the planned action will inevitably be implemented exactly as conceived and on schedule. As a matter of practicality, planning is not a search for ultimate answers but only a means to specific ends that on the proposition that better conditions would result from premeditative as opposed to impulsive actions.

6.1.2   Types of Transportation Planning

Transportation planning is concerned with two separate time horizons. The first is a short-term emphasis intended to select projects that can be implemented within a one-to-three-year period. These projects are designed to provide better management of existing facilities by making them as efficient as possible. The second time horizon deals with the long-rang transportation needs of an area and identifies the projects to be constructed over a 20-year period.

Short-term projects involve programs such as traffic signal timing to improve flow, car and van pooling to reduce congestion, park-and-ride fringe parking lots to increase transit ridership, and transit improvements.

Long-term projects involve programs such as adding new highway elements, additional bus lines or freeway lanes, rapid transit systems and extensions, or access roads to airports or shopping malls.

Transportation planning may take place at any geographical level. In some countries, e.g., the United States, the primary focal point for transportation planning is the metropolitan region, where it is carried out by the Metropolitan Planning Organization (MPO), and is intended to coordinate the activities of local governments, state departments of transportation, and transit operators. In addition, the Intermodal Transportation Efficiency Act (ISTEA, 陆上综合运输效率法) required statewide transportation planning and this requirement continues under subsequent legislation. Also, intercity corridors have sometimes been the focus of planning activity in which alternative ways of providing passenger or freight service between specific pairs of cities are considered.

Transportation planning may involve any transportation mode or combination of modes. Different modes tend to be important at different geographical levels. At the level of the metropolitan region, the primary focus is on the urban passenger modes, that is, highways and mass transit. Local transportation planning also tends to be concerned with urban passenger transportation, but focuses on more detailed issues, while statewide transportation planning activities are apt to give more attention to the allocation of resources among different regions in the state and to intercity transportation, especially freight modes such as trucking or rail.

6.1.3   The Transportation Planning Process

Transportation planning is often portrayed as an orderly and rational process of steps that logically follow one another. In reality, planning and project development are much more complex, often with many different activities occurring concurrently. Shown in Figure 6.1, the planning process starts with understanding the problems facing a community and ends with a solution to identified problems (projects programmed and designed).

In a typical planning context, many of these steps may have already occurred and therefore are not relevant to a particular planning effort. For example, metropolitan planning organizations (MPOs) in the United States have been developing transportation plans for decades, and as a result, a typical planning effort might simply be updating an existing transportation plan. In the context of Figure 6.1, the development of goals, objectives and performance measures might consist of validating those that were developed for the prior version of the plan. Even with these caveats, the planning process shown in Figure 6.1 helps identify important components of the planning process and how they relate to one another.

In practice, transportation planning includes a number of steps as follows:

• monitoring existing conditions;
• forecasting future population and employment growth, including assessing projected land uses in the region and identifying major growth corridors;

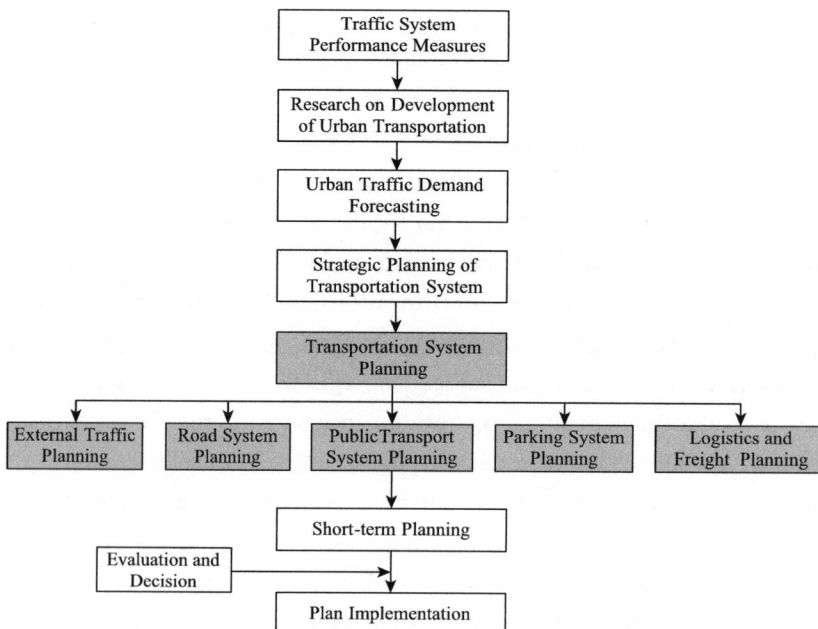

Figure 6.1   Conceptual Framework for Transportation Planning

- identifying current and projected future transportation problems and needs and analyzing, through detailed planning studies, various transportation improvement strategies to address those needs;
- developing long-range plans and short-range programs of alternative capital improvement and operational strategies for moving people and goods;
- estimating the impact of recommended future improvements to the transportation system on environmental features, including air quality;
- developing a financial plan for securing sufficient revenues to cover the costs of implementing strategies.

Urban transportation planning involves the evaluation and selection of highway or transit facilities to serve present and future land uses. For example, the construction of a new shopping center, airport, or convention center will require additional transportation services. Also, new residential development, office space, and industrial parks will generate additional traffic, requiring the creation or expansion of roads and transit services. The transportation planning process must also consider other proposed developments and improvements that will occur within the planning period.

6.2 Transportation Demand Forecasting

6.2.1 Goals of Transportation Demand Forecasting

Demand forecasting is an essential element in the analysis of transportation systems. It is concerned with the behavior of consumers of transportation services and facilities. Users include travelers and shippers of goods in urban, interurban, and international transport markets.

Transportation demand analysis plays several important roles in transportation engineering and planning. These range from attempts to understand the long-range social and environmental implications of decisions about transportation systems to very specific, short-rang predictions of passenger or vehicular flows that are used by designers to size facilities, develop operating and control strategies, and assess the impact of land development and transportation projects.

The goals of transportation demand analysis are to describe travel in meaningful terms, to explain travel behavior, and, on the basis of an understanding of travel behavior, to predict demand for various types of transportation services.

In most cases, the trip is considered to be the basic unit of travel behavior. Trips involve movement from a single origin to a single destination, and are usually described in terms of their origins, destinations, purposes, probability of occurrence, travel modes, and routes. In some cases, more complex units of travel known as trip chains or patterns are studied. These are sets of trips, usually beginning at the traveler's home and proceeding to several destinations in sequence before returning.

6.2.2   Four-Step Forecasting Model

Travel demand in the urban environment refers to the personal travel or passenger trips generated by economic and/or personal needs. Demand for travel is often organized into market segments that reflect a range of factors—including household income, gender, and age of the traveler; auto ownership; and household structure—that influence how many and what kinds of travel activities occur. Transportation supply is represented by the roads, transit facilities and services, information technology, and other infrastructure that enable trips to be made. Transportation supply and travel demand are interdependent—inadequate capacity, which results in congestion, affects travel decisions, and the cumulative effects of individual travelers' decisions affect the performance of the transportation system. Travel demand modeling focuses on this interaction between transportation demand and supply. Given the need for making deliberate, long-term infrastructure investment choices, transportation planners need to know how to model future travel demand and how to interpret the results.

For the past 40 years, transportation professionals have used a four-step approach in modeling transportation demand. Most modeling approaches use some form of these steps today. The major components of travel behavior were identified as follows.

(1) *Trip Generation*

The generation of trips, either from a point of origin or attracted to a destination, is one of the most important components of travel demand modeling. The number of trips generated by each unit of land or type of activity varies according to social, economic, geographic, and land-use factors. Comprehensive studies include estimating both trip productions and trip attractions. Trip productions relate to the home end of the trip, while trip attractions relate to employment or other non-home ends of the trip. Normally, trip productions serve as the control total to which aggregate trip attractions are adjusted.

Both productions and attractions are estimated for different trip types. The most common trip types are home-based work (home to work or work to home), nonhome-based (for example, work to/from shopping) and home-based others (for example, home to/from shopping).

(2) *Trip Distribution*

Trip distribution translates the zonal productions and attractions derived during the trip generation step into origins and destinations, and identifies the impedance (for example, travel time or travel cost) for each origin-destination pair for all zones in the study area. The output of the trip distribution step is an origin-destination (O-D) trip table for all trips by trip purpose.

(3) *Mode Split (Mode Choice)*

Mode choice models are used to predict the number of trips that will use each of the available modes for origin-destination pairs. Modes can include, for example, auto, premium transit, local transit, ridesharing, and walking. Discrete choice models, such as multinomial logit and nested logit models, are the predominant modeling approach used in practice.

(4) *Trip Assignment (Route Choice)*

Trip assignment results in an estimated demand on each of the network links. Link attributes (for example, road or transit line capacity, link length, speed limits, turning restrictions, and travel signals) are represented in the network database and are used to calculate the "cost" of using the link. In its simplest form, this can be measured using the average travel time to traverse the link, or in more sophisticated network models, a generalized cost function is used. In both cases, the network assignment models assign trips through the network to minimize the time or cost of travel.

From Figure 6.2, travel demand models can be chained together in a sequence. In this sequential-demand-modeling arrangement, the outputs of each step become inputs to the following step, which also takes relevant inputs from the specification of the alternative plan under study and from the land-use and socioeconomic projection phase.

What should be attention is that, results of a model are still only estimates—they cannot provide a definitive picture of what will happen in the future. Much like economic projections, transportation forecasts are greatly affected by the long-term economic health and attractiveness of the region, by population changes, and by the individual behavior of each person using the transportation system, which no one can predict.

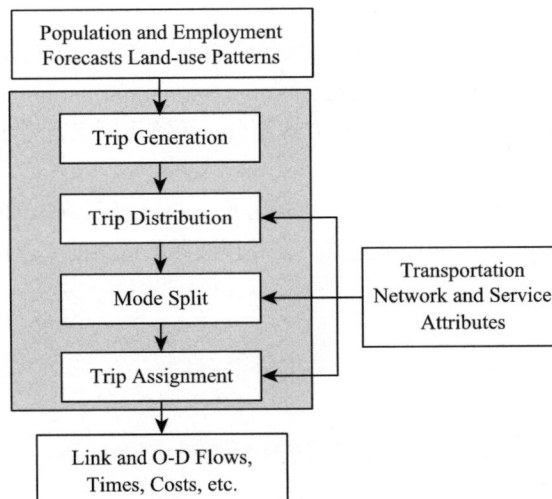

Figure 6.2 The Four Steps in Traditional Travel Demand Modeling

Exercises

1. Describe the goal of transportation planning.

2．Describe the types of transportation planning.
3．Describe the process of transportation planning.
4．What is the goal of transportation demand analysis?
5．What is the four-step forecasting model?

Glossary

1. *Transportation planning*: 交通运输规划，指根据特定交通系统的现状与特征，用科学的方法预测交通运输系统发展趋势，确定特定时期交通供给的建设任务、建设规模及交通系统的管理模式、控制方法，以达到交通系统需求和供给的平衡，实现交通系统的安全、畅通、节能与环保。广义的交通运输规划还包括交通运输基础设施建设发展的规划、交通运输组织管理的规划、生产经营的规划等。
2. *Demand forecasting*: 交通需求预测，是交通规划的核心内容之一，交通发展政策的制定、交通网络设计以及方案评价都与交通需求预测有密切的联系。
3. *Trip generation*: 交通生成预测，预测各交通小区出行的总生成量，包括出行发生预测和出行吸引预测两部分。
4. *Trip distribution*: 交通分布预测，将各交通小区之间的出行发生量和吸引量转化成各交通小区之间的出行交换量。
5. *Mode split (Mode choice)*: 交通方式划分，预测不同出行者出行时选择不同交通工具的比例。
6. *Trip assignment (Route choice)*: 交通分配，将已经预测出的OD交通流按照一定的规则分配到道路网的各条道路上，并预测各条道路的交通量。

Key Points

1．Briefly describe the definition of transportation planning.
简述交通规划的定义。
2．Briefly describe the goals, types and process of transportation planning.
简述交通规划的目标、类型和流程。
3．Briefly describe the purpose of transportation demand forecasting.
简述交通需求预测的目的。
4．Briefly describe the content of the four-stage forecasting model of transportation demand forecasting.
简述交通需求预测四阶段法的内容。

Chapter 7

Intelligent Transportation System

An intelligent transportation system is an area which involves many subjects. It represents the advanced technologies in the whole transportation system. ITS is different from all the other system. Nowadays, the series of systems which use advanced technologies such as computers, information, communication, automatic control, electron and system engineering in order to promote the efficiency of transportation, boost up the safety of road users are called intelligent transportation systems (namely ITS).

7.1   Introduction to ITS

In the work leading to the US Interstate Surface Transportation Efficiency Act (ISTEA, 冰茶法案) legislation in 1991, considerable attention was paid to the advanced technologies that collectively define the elements of ITS. The legislation itself contained directives on ITS, up to and including automated highway demonstrations.

Concurrently, work has been progressing on such systems in many countries, and an international dialog was vital for the efficient incorporation of new technologies and systems. ITS America became a focal point of this, consistent with the intent of the ISTEA legislation.

The ITS emphasis was based on advances over the past few decades in traffic system surveillance and control projects, variable message signing, signal optimization, and simulation.

Perhaps even more important, the emphasis was put in place at a time of a true revolution in computing and communications. Computational cost was decreasing, computer memory was expanding beyond prior concepts, and microprocessors—the heart of the computer—were being integrated into systems ranging from automobiles to dishwashers. At the same time, the availability of a *global positioning system* (*GPS*) enabled the use of *geographic information systems* (*GIS*) so that individuals could locate themselves rather precisely and do it in terms of defined networks, on a global scale. Wireless communication was also becoming widespread, so that cell phones have become commonplace. These devices allow travelers to call for assistance, get advisories, report incidents, and be located (within the bounds within which the data base can be used, under existing law).

This explosion in enabling technologies then focused attention on how transportation systems could be enhanced, building on past work but taking advantage of new, relatively inexpensive and pervasive (普遍的) technological tools.

In the early years of this new focus, there was much attention to standards-setting by government and ITS America: What are the common protocols (协议), interchange formats, and such that should be adopted and used to assure seamless systems?

At the same time, there were major advances in the private sector that acted to preempt (抢先占有) the orderly introduction of such standards: cell phone features and technology are driven by an extremely competitive market; commercial vehicle routing systems became a sales feature in a competitive market and are tailored to customer needs by the private sector; locator and emergency assistance became selling points, as did routing systems; traffic advisories based on Internet-based camera networks became features of regional radio, another competitive private sector market. Cell phone networks have expanded explosively.

With the growing concern over security in the face of terrorism, ITS technology will be extremely relevant, and the range of application (including cargo and passenger inspection) will surely expand.

7.1.1   Definition of ITS

There are a number of similar definitions of ITS available in current publications.

- ITS is the integrated and effective use of advanced technologies in such fields as information, communication, control, sensing and system interoperation on the basis of a complete infrastructure for surface transportation, so as to provide real-time, precise and efficient transport services functioning on wide ranges.
- ITS is an interrelated system that works together to deliver transportation services.
- ITS refers to the use of technology in transportation to save lives, time and money.
- ITS collects, stores, processes information relating to the movement of people and goods.
- ITS is a transport system that applies information, communication, and control technologies to improve the operation of the networks.
- ITS is a collection of systems using advanced technology to facilitate the exchange of information about the overall transportation network between the infrastructure, the users and the operators. This information is used to make effective decisions to safety and efficiency within and as a result of the overall transportation network.

By identifying the common references in these and other published definitions, ITS is such a system which provides the opportunity to integrate travelers, vehicles and infrastructure into a comprehensive system through a range of technologies.

7.1.2   Main Sub-Systems of ITS

An ITS system contains many sub-systems. In this section, we introduce some important sub-systems, which are presented below.

(1) Route Guidance System (RGS)

Route Guidance System (RGS) is different from the Vehicle Navigation System (VNS). RGS will provide drivers with "optimization route" through using computers to analyze traffic conditions of every road in the road network in order to guide drivers to keep away from traffic congestion and choose a light traffic route. RGS can achieve two goals: one is to shorten the delay of road users, another is to make the whole transportation system more smoothly.

(2) Advanced Traffic Management System (ATMS)

ATMS will integrate the management of various roadway functions. It will predict traffic congestion and provide alternative routing instructions to vehicles over regional areas to improve the efficiency of the highway network and maintain priorities for ***high-occupancy vehicles*** (***HOVs***). Real-time data will be collected, utilized and disseminated by ATMS and will further alert transit operators of alternative routes to improve transit operations.

Dynamic traffic control systems will respond in real-time to changing conditions across different jurisdictions (i.e., by routing drivers around accidents). Incident detection will be a critical function in reducing congestion on the nation's highways.

(3) Advanced Traveler Information System (ATIS)

ATIS will provide data to travelers in their vehicles, in their homes or at their homes or at their places of work. Information will include: location of incidents, weather problems, road conditions, optimal routings, lane restrictions, and in-vehicle signing. Information can be provided both to drivers and to transit users and even to people before a trip to help them decide what mode they should use.

(4) Advanced Vehicle Control Systems (AVCS)

AVCS is viewed as an enhancement of the driver's control of the vehicle to make travel both safer and more efficient. AVCS includes a broad range of concepts that will become operational at different time scales, and can provide substantial benefits by improving safety and reducing accident induced congestion.

(5) Automated Highway System (AHS)

When the concepts of AVCS rely more heavily on information and control that could produce improvements in roadways throughout of five to ten times. A new concept called the Automated Highway System (AHS) has engendered. Movements of all vehicles in special lanes would be automatically controlled. One could envision cars running in closely-spaced (headways of less than one foot) platoons of ten or more, at normally highway speed, under automatic control.

(6) Commercial Vehicle Operations (CVO)

In CVO, the private operators of trucks, vans and taxis have already begun to adopt ITS technologies to improve the productivity of their fleets and the efficiency of their operations. This is proving to be a leading-edge application because of direct, bottom-line advantages.

(7) Advanced Public Transportation Systems (APTS)

APTS can use the above technologies to greatly enhance the accessibility of information to users of public transportation as well as to improve the scheduling of public transportation vehicles and the utilization of bus fleets.

(8) Advanced Rural Transportation System (ARTS)

The special economic constraints of relatively low-density roads and the question of how ITS technologies can be applied in this environment are challenges that are being undertaken by many rural areas.

ITS represents a broad set of systemic approaches to transportation. ATMS represents overall network management. ATIS is the provision of information to travelers. AVCS is a new level of control technology applied to vehicles and infrastructure. Applications in urban and rural areas, involving public transportation, commercial vehicles and personal highway vehicles, are encompassed by ITS.

There are important technological issues to be considered, many involving the integration of various hardware and software concepts on a "real-world" transportation network. Few technological "breakthroughs" will be needed.

7.2 Intelligent Vehicle and System

Not only has there been difficulty finding consensus on a name for driverless, autonomous, self-driving, or automated vehicles, there is also the issue of what we actually mean when we say a vehicle is self-driving, automated, and so on.

Do we mean that the vehicle can drive itself anywhere at any time, with no one inside it? Or that the vehicle always needs someone inside ready to take over just in case? Or that the vehicle can drive itself, as long as it is within certain constraints, such as good weather and in a defined area of operations?

In order to bring clarity to this situation, two regulatory bodies covering the United States have defined very similar levels of vehicle automation, with the second bringing greater clarity and now used as the standard.

The first body to define levels was the US Department of Transportation's National Highway Traffic Safety Administration (NHTSA, 美国国家公路交通安全管理局). However, its definition of the most automated level of driving was found to be too broad, and so the SAE International (initially established as the US Society of Automotive Engineers, 美国汽车工程师协会) levels were developed, building on the earlier NHTSA work.

7.2.1　SAE Levels of Driving Automation

The full SAE Levels, which are now the standard in the US and internationally where SAE regulations are observed, are as follows.

- At Level 0, the human driver does everything.
- At Level 1, an automated system on the vehicle can sometimes assist the human driver conduct some parts of the driving task.
- At Level 2, an automated system on the vehicle can actually conduct some parts of the driving task, while the human continues to monitor the driving environment and performs the rest of the driving task.
- At Level 3, an automated system can both actually conduct some parts of the driving task and monitor the driving environment in some instances, but the human driver must be ready to take back control when the automated system requests.
- At Level 4, an automated system can conduct the driving task and monitor the driving environment, and the human need not take back control, but the automated system can operate only in certain environments and under certain conditions.
- At Level 5, the automated system can perform all driving tasks, under all conditions that a human driver could perform them.

With the goal of providing common terminology for automated driving, SAE International's new standard J3016: Taxonomy and Definitions for Terms Related to On-Road Motor Vehicle Automated Driving Systems, delivers a harmonized classification system and supporting definitions that:

- identify six levels of driving automation from "no automation" to "full automation";
- base definitions and levels on functional aspects of technology;
- describe categorical distinctions for a step-wise progression through the levels;
- are consistent with current industry practice;
- eliminate confusion and are useful across numerous disciplines (engineering, legal, media, and public discourse);
- educate a wider community by clarifying for each level what role (if any) drivers have in performing the dynamic driving task while a driving automation system is engaged.

In the formal SAE definition below, note in particular what happens in the shift from SAE 2 to SAE 3: the human driver no longer has to monitor the environment. This is the final aspect of the "dynamic driving task" that is now passed over from the human to the automated system. At SAE 3, the human driver still has the responsibility to intervene when asked to do so by the automated system. At SAE 4 the human driver is relieved of that responsibility and at SAE 5 the automated system will never need to ask for an intervention (Table 7.1).

Table 7.1   Levels of Driving Automation in New SAE International Standard J3016

SAE Level	Name	Narrative Definition	Execution of Steering and Acceleration/ Deceleration	Monitoring of Driving Environment	Fallback Performance of Dynamic Driving Task	System Capability (Driving Modes)
		Human driver monitors the driving environment				
0	No Automation	the full-time performance by the human driver of all aspects of the dynamic driving task, even when *enhanced by warning or intervention systems*	Human driver	Human driver	Human driver	n/a
1	Drive Assistance	the driving mode-specific execution by a driver assistance system of *either steering or acceleration/deceleration* using information about the driving environment and with the expectation that the human driver performs all remaining aspects of the dynamic driving task	Human driver and system	Human driver	Human driver	Some driving modes
2	Partial Automation	the driving mode-specific execution by one or more driver assistance systems of *both steering and acceleration/deceleration* using information about the driving environment and with the expectation that the human driver performs all remaining aspects of the dynamic driving task	System	Human driver	Human driver	Some driving modes
		Automated driving system monitors the driving environment				
3	Conditional Automation	the driving mode-specific performance by an automated driving system of all aspects of the dynamic driving task with the expectation that the *human driver will respond appropriately to a request to intervene*	System	System	Human driver	Some driving modes
4	High Automation	the driving mode-specific performance by an automated driving system of all aspects of the dynamic driving task, *even if a human driver does not respond appropriately to a request to intervene*	System	System	System	Many driving modes
5	Full Automation	the full-time performance by an automated driving system of all aspects of the dynamic driving task *under all roadway and environmental conditions* that can be managed by a human driver	System	System	System	All driving modes

7.2.2   Collaborative Automated Driving System

Collaborative Automated Driving System realizes highway traffic environment with high precision in real time by integrated application of advanced vehicles, intelligent highways with sensing equipment and information interaction (i.e., *I2X* and *V2X*), etc. Collaborative Automated Driving System is constructed from three dimensions: a) vehicle automation, which covers different levels of automated driving; b) network interconnection, with agreed communication protocols and data interaction standards; and c) system integration, which aim to different degrees of collaborative optimization between vehicles, highways and the cloud platform.

Collaborative Automated Driving System is a developing process from low level to high, which includes collaborative perception, collaborative decision, and collaborative control. The system mainly includes the following levels of vehicle-highway-cloud collaborative development: a) Level Ⅰ, vehicle-highway-cloud collaborative perception: vehicle-vehicle, vehicle-highway, vehicle-cloud, and highway-cloud interact and share information; b) Level Ⅱ, collaborative decision: Based on Level Ⅰ, data fusion, state prediction and behavioral decision making can be completed cooperatively; c) Level Ⅲ, collaborative control: Based on Level Ⅰ and Level Ⅱ, collaborative perception, prediction, decision making and collaborative control functions are completed. Transportation system can achieve comprehensive collaboration and support all-weather, all-network and all-light automated driving (Table 7.2).

Table 7.2 Levels of Collaborative Automated Driving System

CAD Level	Vehicle Requirement	Highway Requirement	Communication Requirement	Typical application scenarios
Level I: Collaborative Perception, Drive Assistance	EE* architecture (zonal centralization stage), environment intelligent awareness, interface and human-computer interaction, and information security	Highway detection sensors, multi-dimensional information collection, intelligent road-side equipment, networked traffic signals, basic prediction	V2I and V2V short-range communication, short-range coordination of driving information, vehicle-cloud and highway-cloud telecommunication	Pre-warning driving assistance
Level II: Collaborative Perception, Collaborative Decision	EEI* architecture (central computing stage), environment intelligent awareness, intelligent decision, chassis execution capability, human-computer interaction, and information security function	Updated highway detection sensors, high precision vehicle motion detection sensing, advanced intelligent road-side equipment, networked traffic signals, supporting multi-mode driving	V2I and V2V short-range communication, short-range coordination of driving security information, vehicle-cloud and highway-cloud telecommunication, supporting automated driving bailout	General highway control driving assistance, automated driving on specific roads and closed areas
Level III: Collaborative Perception, Collaborative Decision, Collaborative Control	EEI architecture (vehicle-highway-cloud integration stage) and by-wire chassis, environment intelligence awareness, intelligent decision, human-computer interaction, and information security function	Updated highway detection sensors, intelligent road-side equipment, optimized traffic signals, supporting full vehicle takeover, high-quality intelligent highway system	V2I and V2V short-range communication, advanced short-range information coordination, advanced vehicle-cloud and highway-cloud telecommunication, collaborative perception, decision and control of vehicle-highway-cloud automated driving systems	Multi-vehicle cooperative lane change, signal control optimization, cooperative driving at uncontrolled intersections, and emergency rescue under special conditions, etc.

* EE-Electrical/Electronic Architecture (电子电气架构); EEI-Electrical/Electronic/Information Architecture (电子电气信息架构)

Translated from Reference [20].

Exercises

1. Illustrate the definitions of ITS, GIS, GPS.
2. Describe the main sub-system of ITS.
3. Illustrate levels of automated driving.
4. Describe levels of the Collaborative Automated Driving System.

Glossary

1. *Global positioning system (GPS)*: 全球定位系统，可以在全球范围内实现全天候、实时确定用户的精确位置和精确时间。
2. *Geographic information systems (GIS)*: 地理信息系统，它是在当代技术科学和边缘科学急剧发展的情况下应运而生的，是用来采集、存储、管理、分析和传播空间数据和信息的基础平台。
3. *High-occupancy vehicles (HOVs)*: 合乘车辆，指乘坐2人及以上的乘员（含驾驶员）的车辆。
4. *Collaborative Automated Driving System*: 车路协同自动驾驶系统，是指从信息化、智能化、协同化以及集成化四个维度构建的，利用先进的传感技术、网络技术、计算控制技术及人工智能技术等，能够高效和协同地执行车辆和道路的感知、预测、决策和控制功能，最终形成一个能够整合、协调、控制、管理和优化所有车辆、信息服务、设施设备、智能化交通管理的以智能网联技术为核心的新一代智能交通系统。
5. *I2X: infrastructure to everything*, 基础设施连接一切，实现智能道路基础设施与系统其他部分的双向通信。
6. *V2X: vehicle to everything*, 智能车辆连接一切，实现智能车辆与系统其他部分的双向通信。

Key Points

1. Briefly describe the definition of the intelligent transportation system.
   简述智能交通系统的定义。
2. Briefly describe the sub-systems of the intelligent transportation system.
   简述智能交通系统的子系统。

3. Briefly describe the levels of intelligent vehicles.

   简述智慧车辆的等级。

4. Briefly describe the levels of the Collaborative Automated Driving System.

   简述车路协同自动驾驶系统的等级。

References

[1] Roger P. Roess, Elena S. Prassas, William R. McShane. Traffic Engineering (Fourth Edition). New York: Pearson Education, Inc, 2011.

[2] Michael D. Meyer. Transportation Planning Handbook (Fourth Edition). Institute of Transportation Engineers, John Wiley & Sons, Inc, 2016.

[3] Anurag Pande, Brian Wolshon. Traffic Engineering Handbook (Seventh Edition). Institute of Transportation Engineers, John Wiley & Sons, Inc, 2016.

[4] Michael A. Chacon. Traffic Safety Division Manual: Sign Crew Field Book. Effective Date: October 17, 2018.

[5] 杨孝宽, 贺玉龙. Introduction to Traffic Engineering (Second Edition). 北京: 人民交通出版社有限公司, 2019.

[6] 任福田, 刘小明, 孙立山. 交通工程学（第3版）. 北京: 人民交通出版社股份有限公司, 2017.

[7] 赖元文. 城市交通规划. 北京: 中国建筑工业出版社, 2022.

[8] 邬万江, 马丽丽. 交通工程专业英语. 北京: 机械工业出版社, 2012.

[9] 邬岚. 交通工程专业英语. 北京: 人民交通出版社有限公司, 2016.

[10] 林丽. 交通工程专业英语. 北京: 中国林业出版社, 2012.

[11] 李岩, 王永岗. 交通工程学. 北京: 人民交通出版社有限公司, 2019.

[12] 冯辉荣 李正红. 工程力学. 北京: 中国农业出版社, 2015.

[13] 中华人民共和国主席令(第八号). 中华人民共和国道路交通安全法. 中国法制出版社, 2021.

[14] 中华人民共和国交通运输部, 中华人民共和国公安部. 道路交通标志和标线 第1部分: 总则 GB 5768.1—2009. 中华人民共和国国家质量监督检验检疫总局, 中国国家标准化管理委员会, 2009.

[15] 中华人民共和国交通运输部, 中华人民共和国公安部. 道路交通标志和标线 第2部分: 道路交通标志 GB 5768.2—2022. 国家市场监督管理总局, 国家标准化管理委员会, 2022.

[16] 中华人民共和国交通运输部, 中华人民共和国公安部. 道路交通标志和标线 第3部分: 道路交通标线 GB 5768.3—2009. 中华人民共和国国家质量监督检验检疫总局, 中国国家标准化管理委员会, 2009.

[17] 中华人民共和国公安部. 道路交通管理 机动车类型GA 802—2019. 2019.

[18] 中华人民共和国国务院新闻办公室. 中国交通的可持续发展白皮书. 2020.

[19] 中国公路学会自动驾驶工作委员会, 中国公路学会自动驾驶标准化工作委员会. 车路协同自动驾驶系统分级与智能分配定义与解读报告. 2020.

[20] 中国公路学会, 中国汽车工程学会, 中国通信学会. 车路协同自动驾驶系统协同发展框架. 2023.